# THE ROMERO ROSARY

## JOHN WILSON

PRAYING THE MYSTERIES OF FAITH WITH OUR LADY AND ST OSCAR ROMERO

Graphic Design by Sr Elaine Penrice FSP

| | |
|---|---|
| Cover: | Adobe Stock / #807066928 (From Adobe Express) |
| | & Photo: © Carlos Reyes-Manzo - APA - used with permission of the Archbishop Romero Trust |
| P7 | ©Marcin Mazur / The Romero Cross - St George's Cathedral |
| P8 | ©Romero Trust / Romero praying the rosary |
| P11 | Mitre and Zucchetto of Romero |
| P13 | Romero's blood-stained clothing |
| P14 | Shrine of Romero |
| P15 | Image of Romero on the wall near his residence |
| P16 | Archbishop Romero and Fr Rutilio Grande SJ |
| P19 | St Oscar Romero's Rosary of seeds |
| P21 | Chapel of Divine Providence Cancer Hospital where Romero was assassinated |
| P22 | Rosemary bush in Romero's garden |
| P25 | Bartlomiej Strobel, Public domain, via Wikimedia Commons |

Adobe Express, including a.i. generated images for mysteries of the rosary symbols.

Unless stated, other images are from a private collection, used with permission.

ISBN 9781904785866

Pauline
84 Church Street
Liverlool
L1 3AY

Pauline Books is an expression of the ministry of the Daughters of St Paul,
a charity registered in England and Wales under ref 2960042 and in Scotland under ref SC 037889

Printed by Gutenberg Press Ltd, Gudja Road, Tarxien GXQ 2902 Malta

# THE ROMERO ROSARY

## PRAYING THE MYSTERIES OF FAITH
## WITH OUR LADY AND ST OSCAR ROMERO

## ARCHBISHOP JOHN WILSON

*Archbishop John Wilson was ordained a priest for the Diocese of Leeds in 1995. He was ordained an Auxiliary Bishop in the Diocese of Westminster in 2016 and appointed Archbishop of Southwark in 2019.*

# CONTENTS

# WHY THIS BOOK?

I wonder if you picked up and opened this little book because you love the holy rosary or because you love St Oscar Romero. Perhaps, like me, you love both. Maybe you were just curious about the title. Whatever the reason, thank you. I keep everyone who reads this book in my prayers.

I have prayed the rosary since being a teenager and have been fascinated by the life and witness of St Oscar Romero for the past forty years. These two gifts from God come together here.

©Marcin Mazur / The Romero Cross - St George's Cathedral

I hope what you read inspires you to pray the rosary and to learn more about St Oscar Romero. It is a source of great joy to me, as Archbishop of Southwark, that our Cathedral Church of St George is home to the National Shrine of St Oscar Romero for England and Wales. Every time I walk past the Romero Cross, containing the relics of one of Romero's purple bishop's skull caps (called a zucchetto), and a piece of the vestment he was wearing when he was assassinated, I am reminded of his spiritual closeness. Romero is a saint for our time, faithful to Christ and to the Church, and committed to the defence of human life and dignity. He calls us to love the Lord Jesus and Mary, his Mother, and to put our faith into practice. The rosary is a beautiful way to pray with him, united in spiritual friendship, asking for strength to live out our discipleship today.

I am grateful to those who encouraged me in writing this little book, and to those who provided helpful comments and suggestions. Some words from St Oscar Romero himself capture the spirit of what this book is about:

> "We therefore tell you as we begin the month of the Virgin of the Rosary: let us trust in her, and let us pray hard, sisters and brothers. If the rosary has dropped from your hands, another victim of the secularist tide, remember that as powerful as the tide of worldly secularisation may be, the world will always be in need of prayer and of Mary.

@Romero Trust / Romero praying the rosary

And the more autonomous the world becomes with regard to God, the more compelled those who believe in God will feel to reconnect this world with God, and there is no chain more beautiful for joining the world with God than the chain of the holy rosary."
(Homily, 8 October, 1978)

## WHO IS ST OSCAR ROMERO?

"In Mary we are always referred to Christ. Mary is the sign of Christ's presence. That is why, sisters and brothers, when we say that Mary is the mother of the Church, we are also saying that the Church and Mary are signs of Christ's presence. If the Church saves, it is because she "prolongs the saving mission of Christ. If Mary is the source of inspiration and love in our prayers, it is because she makes visible the power, the tenderness, the redemption of our Lord, Jesus Christ. Mary is the sign of Christ's presence, let us not forget it!" (Homily, 1 January 1978)

## A SAINT, NOT A BYSTANDER

In February 2011, I visited two priests from the Diocese of Leeds working in Peru. One served a parish in Carabayllo on the outskirts of Lima. During my stay, I went out for an early morning walk. I came across a young woman crouching beside the busy highway. Next to her was a large sack of empty metal drink cans. She was running back and forth, in between the traffic, putting the cans in the pathway of oncoming vehicles. Once flattened, she dashed out to retrieve them to sell for recycling. I looked on horrified as she risked her life to earn just a few pennies. Then I noticed a plinth in the central reservation with a bust of Monseñor Romero. He too, as it were, looked on.

The remarkable truth of St Oscar Romero, however, is that he did not just look on at poverty. He was not a bystander when confronted with injustice. His heart burned with empathy and moral indignation. He spoke and he acted. Before he was ever martyred or canonised, he lived as an apostle and preached like a prophet.

## BEGINNING WITH MARY

Oscar Romero - Oscar Arnulfo Romero y Galdámez, to give his full name - was born on 15 August 1917 in Ciudad Barrios. This small town, situated in the San Miguel region of eastern El Salvador, calls itself the 'cuna' - the cradle - of Monseñor Romero. His statues, in the Parish Church and the Town Square, signal the continuing esteem his own people have towards him.

Romero was the second of eight children born to his father, Santos Romero, and his mother, Guadalupe de Jesús Galdámez. From the beginning, Romero had a special relationship with Our Lady. His birthday, the 15 August, is the Feast of her Assumption into heaven. From early childhood, he nurtured a devotion to the Blessed Virgin Mary, Mother of God, especially through the rosary.

After primary school, and a short apprenticeship as a carpenter, the young Oscar, aged just 13, entered the minor seminary in San Miguel. In January 1937, he began his studies for the priesthood at the major seminary in the capital, San Salvador. Shortly afterwards, he was transferred to the Latin American College in Rome. Following priestly ordination in Rome on 4 April 1942, Romero remained in the Eternal City to pursue doctoral studies in spiritual theology.

## LIFE AS A PRIEST

The global uncertainty of the Second World War caused Romero's bishop to recall his young priest back to El Salvador in 1943. Detained in Cuba for three months on the journey home, Romero eventually celebrated Mass in his hometown for the first time on 11 January 1944. He then began his parish pastoral ministry.

Fr Romero served initially in the Parish of Our Lady, Virgin of the Assumption, in Anamorós, towards the eastern border with Honduras. A further assignment followed quickly, to the Cathedral Parish of San Miguel, where he ministered for more than two decades. In addition to his sacramental ministry, Romero showed his solidarity with people in need, for example, supporting poor coffee pickers and shoeshine boys. He was also chaplain to groups such as the Legion of Mary, the Honour Guard of the Blessed Sacrament, and the Holy Rosary Association. Romero lived happily among the ordinary people and worked hard as their shepherd. From his early years as a priest, he began to establish an impressive reputation as a preacher.

Romero's qualities and skills soon gained attention. Appointed General Secretary of the Bishops' Conference of El Salvador in 1966, he received the honorific title

'Monsignor,' Monseñor in Spanish. He lodged at the major seminary in San Salvador and became friends with the Jesuit Fr Rutilio Grande who served on the seminary staff. This friendship would be highly significant for Romero later in life.

## NOMINATION AS A BISHOP

On 24 April 1970, the Holy See announced Mgr Romero's nomination as an auxiliary bishop for the Archdiocese of San Salvador. He received episcopal ordination the following 21 June and his friend, Fr Grande, was the liturgical Master of Ceremonies. Just under three and a half years later, on 15 October 1974, Pope Paul VI entrusted Bishop Romero with the leadership of the rural Diocese of Santiago de Maria. This new responsibility enabled Bishop Romero to root himself more deeply in the pastoral accompaniment of his people. He was sensitive to the harsh conditions of the poorest, notably those working on coffee plantations.

Political tensions in El Salvador, between the powerful and the powerless, were a source of escalating tension, and of concern to Bishop Romero. Although shy and reserved by nature, and given to anxiety, he found a voice to speak against violence and injustice, becoming 'a voice for the voiceless.'

## APPOINTMENT AS ARCHBISHOP

Bishop Romero received news of his appointment as Archbishop of San Salvador on 3 February 1977. It was a time of national crisis. There was a wealthy ruling elite, a militarised government, and a poor oppressed working class. In response, some had turned to guerrilla warfare. Following a

*Mitre and Zucchetto of Romero*

manipulated presidential election on 20 February 1977, the government deployed military forces to suppress legitimate protests. Into this brutal state of affairs stepped the new Archbishop, not entirely welcomed by everyone.

Newly installed, Archbishop Romero chose to live within the grounds of the Hospital of Divine Providence run by the Missionary Carmelite Sisters of St Teresa. He took up residence, very modestly, in the one room sacristy adjacent to the chapel. It became his bedroom and study, with a tiny bathroom attached. His choice of accommodation signalled his desire to share the living conditions of his people. It also indicated, perhaps, a certain discomfort with his elevated position. The new Archbishop wanted to keep in touch with reality, not living, as it were, up in the trees, but with his feet firmly on the ground. However, his living quarters soon proved impractical. He could only meet people in the chapel. After living a few months in the sacristy, the sisters built him a three-roomed bungalow in the grounds of the hospital giving him space to work properly and hold meetings with privacy.

## THE KILLING OF FR GRANDE

On Saturday 12 March 1977, Archbishop Romero's friend, Fr Rutilio Grande SJ, was assassinated, along with Nelson Lemus (aged 16) and Manuel Solorzano (aged 72). They were travelling from Aguilares to El Paisnal, to celebrate a novena Mass to St Joseph. Death squad gunmen had hidden themselves in the sugar-cane fields beside the narrow dusty road. About 5.30 pm, they fired on Fr Grande's car killing the priest and two laymen. Their martyrdom made a great impact on Romero. He went immediately to the Church where the three bodies lay before the altar. To emphasise the enormity of events, a week later, Sunday 20 March, Romero permitted only one Mass in the Archdiocese - 'La Misa Unica' – celebrated in front of the Cathedral. Over 100,000 people attended.

Throughout his ministry, Archbishop Romero spoke against injustice and violence in El Salvador. Inspired by the Second Vatican Council, he read the signs of the times in the light of the Gospel of Christ. Through homilies and pastoral messages, he interpreted the tragic experience of the people he loved through the teaching of Scripture and the Church. As he became more outspoken against oppression, so the threats to his life increased. In his Sunday homily on 23 March 1980, Romero demanded that soldiers refuse to obey any orders to kill innocent people. For those in power, this was the last straw.

## ROMERO'S MARTYRDOM

On 24 March 1980, while celebrating Holy Mass, Archbishop Romero was assassinated aged 62. He was martyred 'in odium fidei,' in hatred of the faith, not as a soldier or a politician, but as a prophetic shepherd. In faithfulness to Christ and his Gospel, Romero could not remain silent while his own people faced repression, torture, and murder. His death provoked outrage and condemnation around the world. It broke the hearts of so many people in El Salvador for whom he was a father, friend, and defender against the wolves.

Romero's funeral Mass took place six days later, on Sunday 30 March. It happened to be Palm Sunday that year, when we remember the triumphal entry of the Lord Jesus into Jerusalem to undergo his passion and death, from which he would rise again. The enormous crowd that gathered in front of San Salvador Cathedral was attacked with explosives and gunfire. In the chaos that followed, the funeral Mass could not continue. With haste, Romero's coffin was buried in a temporary tomb in the Cathedral crypt.

*Romero's blood-stained clothing*

## THE ROAD TO SAINTHOOD

*Shrine of Romero*

Despite various obstacles along the way, Archbishop Romero's cause for sainthood made slow progress. In Rome, Pope St John Paul II expressed his impatience at the delays. Pope Benedict XVI worked to 'unblock' the remaining difficulties and Pope Francis approved his Beatification. Romero was declared 'Blessed' in San Salvador on 23 May 2015. Three and a half years later, he was canonised by Pope Francis on 14 October 2018 in St Peter's Square, Rome. His feast day is 24 March.

Since 2005, St Oscar Romero's body has rested in a new rectangular tomb in the Cathedral crypt, fashioned beautifully in bronze. Romero is represented sleeping the sleep of the just. The tomb's symbolism speaks of his life. Statues of the four Gospel writers, Saints Matthew, Mark, Luke, and John stand, one on each corner, each carrying a copy of their Gospels. Images of Romero's head and hands are visible, as it were, reaching out from the grave. Romero's mitred head has been worn smooth, polished by people's hands as they seek to connect tangibly with him. One of his hands holds the crozier - also polished through people's touch. The other hand holds the palm branch of martyrdom. A red ball of jasper, the colour of martyrdom, marks the site of the gunshot wound close to his heart. There is an olive branch, the symbol of peace; and there are roses, representing his devotion to Our Lady, Queen of Peace the petals signifying life and beauty, the thorns signifying pain and suffering.

## ST OSCAR ROMERO'S IMPACT AND LEGACY

Looking back at St Oscar Romero's life, we see someone, above all, given over completely to Christ: as a disciple, priest, bishop, and, finally, as a martyr. We cannot understand him separated from his impassioned stance for justice, his brave defence of human rights, his relentless advocacy for the poor, and his rejection of oppression and violence. Romero spoke and acted in this way because he belonged to Christ and he believed the Gospel. He knew that what was happening before his eyes, to the weakest and the poorest, was happening to Christ and to his afflicted body, the Church.

Romero's rise as a champion of God-given human dignity was not due to a specific 'conversion' at a determined point. Rather, he experienced a growing awareness, an evolution of pastoral strengthening and understanding, according to the demands of the Gospel and the plight of so many of his fellow citizens. As Christ crucified shared our sufferings, so, increasingly, Romero entered the suffering of his people. He could not, and would not, simply look on. Here was a shepherd who not only smelled of his sheep, but who shed his blood with and for them while celebrating Holy Mass, united to the sacrifice of Christ.

*Image of Romero on the wall near his residence*

Humanly speaking, Romero was a nervous man, an introvert who worried and struggled. 'God knows how hard it was for me to become archbishop,' he said in February 1978, 'how timid I have felt before you, except for the support that you as the Church have given me. You have made your bishop a sign of Christianity.' (Homily, 5 February 1978) Romero drew strength from his deep interior relationship with the Lord Jesus and from his people. He inspires us to follow Christ, trying, as he did, to put the Gospel into action in the situations we face. He inspires us to believe in the salvation Christ won for us from sin and death. He points the way, through faith and discipleship, towards holiness and heaven. Yet, he also knew there was an earthly consequence to Christ's offer of divine redemption, made to each one of us. It concerns how we live in the present moment, and how we put into practice the commandments of God's kingdom. 'Those who do not understand transcendence,' said Romero, 'cannot understand us. When we speak of injustice here below and denounce it, they think we are playing politics. It is in the name of God's just reign that we denounce the injustices of earth.' (Homily, 2 September 1979) With the Gospel as our compass, Romero pushes us to ask how we are really acting and speaking against injustice and in defence of the poor.

Romero believed that every person is capable of making a difference for the better, towards others and towards our world. He took Christ at his word. When the Lord Jesus said, 'Whatever you do to the least of my brothers and sisters, you do this to me,' (Mt 25:40) Romero said, 'Amen' - I believe it. This truth sculpted his life, so much so that, in imitation of Christ, he could literally lay down his life for his friends.

Both during and after his lifetime, ruthless conflict in El Salvador left Romero's homeland wounded and scarred. The civil war saw around 75,000 civilians killed, including approximately 8,000 'disappeared people' taken and never seen again. Death squads murdered countless innocent people, including priests, religious sisters, and laity. Among so many victims, the names of Fr Rutilio Grande SJ, Manuel Solorzano, Nelson Lemus, Sr Maura Clarke MM, Sr Ita Ford MM, Sr Dorothy Kazel

OSU, Jean Donovan, Fr Cosme Spessotto OFM, and the six Jesuit priests and two lay women massacred at the Central American University, all shape the Salvadoran martyrology.

In terrible years of darkness and turmoil, faith remained Romero's anchor. 'Christianity's only true absolute,' he said, '[is] God and his Christ.' (Homily, 18 September 1977) In changing times, he preached a changeless truth: God in Christ is with us, 'a pilgrim accompanying us throughout history.' (Homily, 18 March 1979)

'There is no liberation,' preached Romero, 'without the cross. There are no true liberators without hope in another life.' (Homily, 16 April 1978) Hope in Christ's victory over death, the forgiveness of sins, and the commandment to love and to live the Gospel, all this, and more, gives purpose and meaning to our authentic existence and destiny. Romero stood beside the marginalised and dispossessed. He knew Christian love has no expiry date or exclusions. Like him, we must strive to be Christ to whomever we meet on the road. Our life together is a pilgrimage, something holy that leads us to God.

Archbishop Romero and Fr Rutilio Grande SJ

Romero was not indifferent towards injustice, poverty, and violence. Christ directed his response and the Gospel was his roadmap. He accompanied and he listened. He unpacked the Scriptures and gathered people around the altar. Faith in the risen Christ gave him strength to stand firm and preach ongoing conversion here and now. Conversion to peace and reconciliation. Conversion to respect for human life and dignity. Conversion to sharing fairly the earth's resources. Conversion to genuine freedom as God's children. Minutes before that fatal bullet struck Romero he declared: 'God's reign is already present on our earth in mystery. When the Lord comes, it will be brought to perfection. That is the hope that inspires Christians. We know that every effort to better society, especially when injustice and sin are so ingrained, is an effort that God blesses, that God wants, that God demands of us.' (Homily, 24 March 1980) In the service of God's kingdom and the sometimes daunting search for truth, holiness, justice, love, and peace, God commands that we speak and act, not just look on in passive silence.

St Oscar Romero invites us to an ever-deepening relationship with Christ through the Church. He calls us to the sacraments and the life of faith. He forbids us to seek benefit or profit at the expense of anyone else. He asks us to walk forward in virtuous harmony with as many people as possible, especially those on the margins. He urges us to give what we can, to do what we can, and to say what we can, to make a difference to those most in need.

Archbishop Romero's cassocks still hang in his wardrobe. Their length shows he was shorter in physical height, but he was a giant in spiritual stature. Christ called him to greatness in the service of others. This is why he remains relevant to the world today. His legacy is a summons to witness that selfishness - whether personal, or societal, national or international - only ever brings division, even destruction and death. Self-giving, however, always yields life, even when that self-gift is a sacrificial grain of wheat which dies in the soil to produce a rich harvest.

This inspirational saint of the twentieth century Church was so completely open to Christ, to the prompting of the Holy Spirit, to overcoming his personal insecurities, and to preaching the word of life so powerfully, that, like his Saviour, it cost him everything. St Oscar Romero did God's will through faithfulness to Christ and by loving as Christ commanded. May his example and heavenly intercession grant us something of the same in the cause of justice, peace, and the service of our sisters and brothers in need.

## THE ROMERO ROSARY

Having heard something of St Oscar Romero's story, we turn to the main purpose of this book, which is twofold. First, to help us pray with, and to, Our Lady - with St Oscar - so that we might grow in our love and service of Christ and each other; and second, to draw us into friendship with St Oscar through familiarity with his words of preaching. The means to do this, as presented here, is through the rosary. Using the Scriptures and St Oscar's words, we will explore the traditional mysteries of joy, light, sorrow, and glory. Then we will move to consider what I have called the Romero mysteries of charity, of compassion and mercy, and of justice and peace.

*St Oscar Romero's Rosary of seeds*

# INTRODUCING THE ROMERO ROSARY

"The mysteries of the rosary are a precious summary of the Gospel. This is understood even by little children who count the beads of the rosary in their tiny hands while they meditate on the Child Jesus, on the Jesus who dies for us, on the risen Jesus, and on the Virgin who accompanies this Christ in his childhood, in his agonies, and in his resurrection. Those who pray the rosary while recalling these Gospel mysteries become Christians in the best of schools, the school of the Virgin who is the best Christian." (Homily, 2 October 1977)

## THE ROSARY, ROSEMARY, AND ST OSCAR ROMERO

Anyone who, like me, has worked in Catholic prison chaplaincy will be familiar with requests from people in prison for a rosary. The rosaries distributed in prisons usually have beads moulded from plastic. Some even glow in the dark. A person in prison once shared with me how comforting it was, if he woke up troubled during the night, to see his rosary glowing beside his bed. On more than one occasion, however, the request came not for rosary beads, but for rosemary beads! It is a lovely slip of the tongue, and one relevant to this little book of rosary devotions connected with St Oscar Romero. The name Romero is also the Spanish word for rosemary. So, when people in prison asked for 'rosemary beads,' they were, in a sense, asking for Romero beads!

## ENCOUNTERING ARCHBISHOP ROMERO

I first encountered Archbishop Romero when I was 17, long before I became a priest, let alone an Archbishop. I bought a book called 'The Church is All of You,' edited by Fr James Brockman SJ. It presented a selection of thoughts and quotations from Romero's homilies and speeches. His life and witness fascinated me. Never could I have imagined, thirty-five years later in 2023, that I would have the privilege of visiting El Salvador myself on pilgrimage in the footsteps of St Oscar Romero.

The trip began with a visit to what had been Archbishop Romero's modest residence in the grounds of the 'Hospitalito,' the Divine Providence Cancer Hospital in San Salvador. His former home stands today as a shrine, just two minutes' walk from the hospital chapel, the site of his assassination on 24 March 1980, around 6:30 pm, while celebrating a memorial Requiem Mass.

*Chapel of Divine Providence Cancer Hospital where Romero was assassinated*

The chapel was smaller than I imagined. Behind the altar, on the sanctuary floor, there is a life-sized outline of Romero's body showing where he collapsed and died. The inscription on the sanctuary wall, beside the crucifix, reads 'At this altar Mons Oscar Romero offered his life to God for his people.' I celebrated the Eucharist standing in exactly the same place Romero stood when he was killed, the silhouette of his bloodied body beneath my feet.

Standing on the spot where Archbishop Romero's life was ended put his life and my own into relationship and perspective. Memory, loss, sadness, and reality, all intertwine as we sense the enormity of our living and dying. From behind the altar of the hospital chapel, there is a clear view of the main entrance. Romero would have seen the car arrive and the gunman get out and point the gun towards him. His martyrdom was a Christ-like sacrifice. In a split-second movement from Gethsemane to Calvary, Romero saw his death unfold before his eyes. The exploding bullet penetrated his chest, just above his heart. The fatal injury caused massive internal bleeding. Romero died in the arms of the people he loved and served, faithful to the end.

## ROSEMARY FOR REMEMBRANCE

In Shakespeare's dramatic tragedy Hamlet, the character of Ophelia, a young noblewoman from Denmark, declares, 'There's rosemary, that's for remembrance: pray, love, remember.'

*Rosemary bush in Romero's garden*

At the time of Archbishop Romero's beatification, given that in Spanish the name Romero is also the word for rosemary, there was a saying, a play on words: 'Sow a seed of rosemary in your garden, and sow a seed of Romero in your heart.'

Romero's episcopal coat of arms displays three sprigs of flowering rosemary. Still today, the little garden in front of his small house has flourishing rosemary bushes around a grotto of Our Lady of Lourdes. It was to the poor child, Bernadette Soubirous, aged just fourteen, that Our Lady appeared at the Grotto of Massabielle in Lourdes in 1858. During each of the eighteen apparitions, between 11 February and 16 July that year, Our Lady prayed the rosary with little Bernadette. The message and power of the rosary was close to Romero's heart.

## ROMERO'S ROSARY

St Oscar's former home as Archbishop of San Salvador is striking in its simplicity. It remains much the same as he left it the day he set off to celebrate Mass, never to return. His books sit on the shelves. His belongings are in the wardrobe. On his desk are his typewriter and the tape recorder he used to record his diary. The bloodstained shirt and vestments, worn the day he was martyred, are all on display. With these, in a glass-topped cabinet, together with his pectoral cross and a purple zucchetto, rests his rosary, a simple cross and chain with white beads.

The rosary was an essential part of Romero's daily prayer. As a young priest, he prayed the rosary in the evening with the people in the parish. On long journeys, he prayed it many times over. His driver, Juan Bosco Palacios, recounts how in moments of terrible crisis, when he was most anxious, Archbishop Romero would always turn to his rosary.

What he learnt as a child became part of his spiritual life as a priest, bishop, and archbishop. This familiar prayer brought him great consolation on the many dark days when he, with his people, faced animosity and threat.

During his time as Archbishop, Romero encouraged the people of San Salvador in their prayerful affection towards Our Lady:

*Image / Adobe Express*

"The simplicity of our rosary, the simplicity of our pilgrimages to Mary's shrines, our visits to the images of Mary - why not fall on our knees? We don't do this with a sense of idolatry, but with the same tenderness with which we often kneel before our mothers in order to speak with them more intimately. ... What I wish for, sisters and brothers, is for there to be a renewal in our archdiocese of this devotion that is so traditional and proverbial among our families. In many homes the rosary is no longer prayed, and in many families the name of Mary is no longer invoked. And forgive me for saying this, dear Christian communities, but in your communities I have often felt sad when you offer beautiful, spontaneous prayers to God and to Christ, but do not mention Mary. Let us renew our awareness of her presence because her presence is a sign that Christ is near, that he is with us." (Homily, 1 Jan 1978)

And again:

> "I want to echo the pope's insistence that we Catholics be very devoted to the Blessed Virgin Mary and that we pray the rosary frequently if possible." (Homily, 13 May 1979)

## WRITING ABOUT ROMERO AND THE ROSARY

When appointed a bishop, Romero took as his episcopal motto *Sentire Cum Ecclesia* (Latin), or *Sentir Con La Iglesia* (Spanish). It means to sense or perceive with the Church's faith; to feel and understand life from within the Church according to her belief in Christ. Signalling something more than a purely intellectual grasp of faith, Romero's motto speaks of living one's faith attentive to the mind of the Church, in communion with one's brothers and sisters in Christ. As a priest and bishop, Romero held together a remarkable love for the Church and an increasingly passionate defence of the poor. He combined fidelity to Church teaching with a courageous critique of injustice. While some misinterpreted him as a purely political liberator, he remained a truly faithful shepherd of God's Church on behalf of God's people.

There are those who might admire Romero's advocacy of social justice, but not appreciate his ecclesial consciousness and spirituality, including his devotion to Our Lady and the rosary. Others might pray the rosary, but feel no connection with St Oscar and his witness for human dignity and rights. This little book seeks to connect the prayerful beauty of the rosary with St Oscar's compelling words. Quotations from his homilies accompany each mystery of the rosary. I hope it will appeal to those who love the rosary, those who love Romero, and those who love both. There is, however, something more offered here.

## THE ROSARY IN THE CHURCH

Praying the rosary has a long tradition in the Church. In the early 1200s, St Dominic had a vision in which Our Lady gave him the rosary and its prayers. Ever since, sinners and saints, royalty and paupers, have treasured this powerful prayer. The rosary is a universally accessible way of praying. Anyone can pray it, uniting spiritually with Mary, the Mother of Jesus, asking her help to come closer to her Son. Through his Blessed Mother's eyes, we contemplate the events of our Lord's saving life, death, and resurrection.

As a seminarian in Rome, I participated in a retreat given by Cardinal Basil Hume who served as Archbishop of Westminster from 1976 to 1999. In a sermon during the retreat, he offered one of the simplest, yet most encouraging explanations of the rosary I have ever heard. The Cardinal invited us to imagine sitting down next to a woman as she talks through a photo album of pictures portraying the important events in the life of her son. She shares with

*Our Lady of the Rosary with St. Dominic and St. Nicholas*

you her first-hand witness of what happened to him, both the happy times and the sad times. The more she speaks about him, the more you get to know him. After she has finished talking with you, you know her son much better than before you started. This is because of her unique relationship with him, which, through her, you share more fully. All this happens, said Cardinal Hume, when we pray the rosary.

# THE MYSTERIES OF THE ROSARY

Until recently, there were traditionally three sets of mysteries (or overarching themes) of the holy rosary: joy, sorrow, and glory. Each of these has five particular mysteries attached based on events taken from the life of the Lord Jesus and Our Lady.

## THE MYSTERIES OF JOY

Under the overarching mystery (or theme) of joy, there are five joyful mysteries concerning events from the Lord Jesus' birth and childhood:

1. The Annunciation to Mary of the Birth of the Lord Jesus
2. The Visitation of Mary to her Cousin Elizabeth
3. The Birth of the Lord Jesus in Bethlehem
4. The Presentation of the Lord Jesus in the Temple
5. The Finding of the Lord Jesus in the Temple

## THE MYSTERIES OF SORROW

Under the overarching mystery (or theme) of sorrow, there are five sorrowful mysteries concerning events from the Lord Jesus' passion and death:

1. The Agony of the Lord Jesus in the Garden of Gethsemane
2. The Scourging of the Lord Jesus at the Pillar
3. The Crowning of the Lord Jesus with Thorns
4. The Lord Jesus Carries his Cross
5. The Crucifixion and Death of the Lord Jesus

## THE MYSTERIES OF GLORY

Under the overarching mystery (or theme) of glory, there are five glorious mysteries concerning events from the Lord Jesus' victory over death and the life of heaven:

1. The Resurrection of the Lord Jesus from the Dead
2. The Ascension of the Lord Jesus into Heaven
3. The Descent of the Holy Spirit on the Apostles at Pentecost
4. The Assumption of Our Blessed Lady, Body and Soul, into Heaven
5. The Coronation of Our Blessed Lady in Heaven and the Glory of All the Saints

In 2002, St John Paul II added a new set of mysteries of light to the existing mysteries of joy, sorrow, and glory. These luminous mysteries include events from the Gospels about Christ's public ministry between his baptism and his passion. St John Paul II presented this to the Church in the Apostolic Letter *Rosarium Virginis Mariae* (RVM) - On the Most Holy Rosary of the Virgin Mary - a wonderful reflection on the rosary within Catholic spirituality and worthwhile reading.

## THE MYSTERIES OF LIGHT

Under the overarching mystery (or theme) of light, there are five luminous mysteries concerning events from the Lord Jesus' public ministry:

1. The Baptism of the Lord Jesus in the River Jordan
2. The Miracle at the Wedding Feast at Cana
3. The Proclamation of the Kingdom of God and the Call to Conversion
4. The Transfiguration of the Lord
5. The Institution of the Holy Eucharist

# THE ROMERO MYSTERIES

Taking a lead from St John Paul II, and inspired by St Oscar Romero, I offer here for prayerful consideration and devotion, alongside the four sets of mysteries of joy, light, sorrow, and glory, three new sets of mysteries: the mysteries of charity, the mysteries of compassion and mercy, and the mysteries of justice and peace. We might call them the 'Romero mysteries' - being mysteries of loving service and solidarity, themes which stand at the core of our discipleship and all our relationships.

## THE MYSTERIES OF CHARITY

Under the overarching mystery (or theme) of charity there are five, what might be called, charitable mysteries. These events reveal the command of the Lord Jesus to show unconditional love for every person, something which every disciple is called to put into practice.

1.  The Lord Jesus Teaches Love for Enemies
2.  The Lord Jesus Gives the Great Commandment
3.  The Lord Jesus Calls us to Imitate the Good Samaritan
4.  The Lord Jesus Washes his Disciples' Feet and gives the New Commandment
5.  The Lord Jesus Recommissions the Apostle Peter

## THE MYSTERIES OF COMPASSION AND MERCY

Under the overarching mystery (or theme) of compassion and mercy, there are five compassionate and merciful mysteries. These events exemplify the tender-hearted attitude and teaching of the Lord Jesus which we are called to embrace and live out in daily life.

1. The Lord Jesus Calls Matthew the Tax Collector
2. The Woman Anoints the Feet of the Lord Jesus
3. The Lord Jesus Encounters the Rich Young Man
4. The Lord Jesus Meets the Woman Caught in Adultery
5. The Lord Jesus Teaches About the Prodigal Son and the Forgiving Father

## THE MYSTERIES OF JUSTICE AND PEACE

Under the overarching mystery (or theme) of justice and peace, there are five just and peaceful mysteries. These events illustrate the mission of the Lord Jesus to foster love, justice, and peace, signs of God's kingdom which we are called to bring to life.

1. The Lord Jesus Speaks in the Synagogue at Nazareth
2. The Lord Jesus Imparts the Beatitudes
3. The Lord Jesus Calls Zacchaeus to Conversion
4. The Lord Jesus Teaches about the Final Judgement
5. The Risen Lord Jesus Brings the Gift of Peace

As you will see, this book presents all seven sets of rosary mysteries, each with a summary of the relevant passage from the Scriptures, with quotations from Romero's preaching, with questions for reflection, and a simple prayer. I hope these will help to lead us, through the truths of our faith, closer to the Lord Jesus and his Blessed Mother. I pray too that they will also help us to deepen our appreciation of St Oscar's life, teaching, and witness, as we find in him a spiritual companion and intercessor.

Pope St John Paul II described the rosary in these words:

> "The Rosary is by its nature a prayer for peace, since it consists in the contemplation of Christ, the Prince of Peace, the one who is 'our peace.' (Eph 2:14) Anyone who assimilates the mystery of Christ - and this is clearly the goal of the Rosary - learns the secret of peace and makes it his life's project. Moreover, by virtue of its meditative character, with the tranquil succession of Hail Marys, the Rosary has a peaceful effect on those who pray it, disposing them to receive and experience in their innermost depths, and to spread around them, that true peace which is the special gift of the Risen Lord. (cf. Jn 14:27; 20.21)" (RVM, 40)

We can add to these some powerful words from St Oscar Romero:

> "We have great devotion to the Virgin, sisters and brothers, but it's a liberating devotion, a devotion that helps us learn from Mary the freedom with which she spoke. Our devotion to the Virgin should make us feel close to God, but not with the intention of imposing our way of thinking or our false prudence. Our devotion should make us stand up for Christ when he is nailed to the cross by the world's injustice and when everyone flees except Mary, who stays there beside him. She is the courageous woman ... who defends the rights of God and the rights of humans even when the cost is humiliation and danger." (Homily, 15 July 1979)

# HOW TO PRAY THE ROSARY

"And we recommend that everyone pray the holy rosary as an expression of the life of Christian communities and Christian families." (Homily, 8 October, 1978)

## PRAYING THE MYSTERIES OF FAITH

We use the rosary to pray one of the sets of mysteries: either one of the traditional mysteries of joy, light, sorrow, or glory, or one of the sets of Romero mysteries of charity, compassion and mercy, or justice and peace. As noted previously, each of these has an overarching mystery and then a set of five particular mysteries.

## THE SHAPE AND STRUCTURE OF THE ROSARY

A rosary is a specially constructed circular string of beads or knots, fixed on a chain or a cord. Rosaries come in all shapes and sizes and are made from various materials. Every rosary, however, has the same basic structure to help us to pray.

While there are some variations in the additional prayers in use when praying the rosary, the essential prayers always follow the same pattern. The outline given here relates to the material contained in the following sections of this book. This includes the message of the Scriptures, quotations from St Oscar Romero, questions for reflection, and a prayer.

## BEGINNING THE ROSARY

Attached to the circular string of beads is a crucifix or a cross. This is the place to begin the rosary. Decide which set of mysteries of the rosary you wish to pray. Make the Sign of the Cross - in the name of the Father, and of the Son, and of the Holy Spirit, Amen - and announce the title of the mysteries - for example, 'The Five Joyful

Mysteries of the Holy Rosary' - aloud if praying with a group, or silently, as appropriate. Then, holding the crucifix, recite the Apostles' Creed.

> I believe in God,
> the Father Almighty,
> Creator of heaven and earth,
> and in Jesus Christ, His only Son, our Lord,
> who was conceived by the Holy Spirit,
> born of the Virgin Mary,
> suffered under Pontius Pilate,
> was crucified, died and was buried;
> He descended into hell;
> on the third day He rose again from the dead;
> He ascended into heaven,
> and is seated at the right hand of God the Father Almighty;
> from there He will come to judge the living and the dead.
> I believe in the Holy Spirit,
> the Holy Catholic Church,
> the communion of Saints,
> the forgiveness of sins,
> the resurrection of the body,
> and life everlasting. Amen.

Moving down the chain, away from the crucifix,
pray the Our Father on the next bead.

> Our Father who art in heaven,
> hallowed be Thy name.
> Thy kingdom come.
> Thy will be done on earth,
> as it is in heaven.

Give us this day our daily bread,
and forgive us our trespasses,
as we forgive those who trespass against us,
and lead us not into temptation,
but deliver us from evil. Amen.

Then on each of the next three beads pray the Hail Mary.
Sometimes, three intentions accompany these three Hail Marys - for an increase in
faith, in hope, and in love.

Hail, Mary, full of grace,
the Lord is with thee.
Blessed art thou among women
and blessed is the fruit of thy womb, Jesus.
Holy Mary, Mother of God,
pray for us sinners,
now and at the hour of our death. Amen.

After the three Hail Marys, pray the Glory be.
This does not have its own particular bead.

Glory be to the Father
and to the Son
and to the Holy Spirit,
as it was in the beginning,
is now, and ever shall be,
world without end. Amen.

The Our Father, three Hail Marys, and Glory be
are also sometimes offered for the Pope and his intentions.

## PRAYING THE MYSTERIES

Announce, or consider silently, the first of the five particular mysteries of this set of mysteries, such as 'The Baptism of the Lord Jesus in the River Jordan' if praying the mysteries of light. When using this book, for a reflective praying of the rosary, read the message from the Scriptures and then the words from St Oscar Romero (either one or both quotations). Consider the reflection questions and say the prayer.

Each particular mystery is called a decade (because of the ten Hail Marys). Begin praying the Our Father on the single bead, then ten Hail Marys, prayed on the next ten beads, followed by the Glory be. Some people then add the Fatima Prayer: O my Jesus, forgive us our sins, save us from the fires of hell; lead all souls to Heaven, especially those who have most need of your mercy. Neither the Glory be, nor the Fatima Prayer, has its own particular bead.

Repeat this pattern for each of the other four particular mysteries within the overarching mystery, passing the beads through your fingers as you go. If you are new to praying the rosary, this may seem a little unusual or mechanical at first, but it soon becomes second nature.

At the end of the fifth decade, say the following prayers:

> Hail, Holy Queen, Mother of Mercy,
>   Hail our life, our sweetness and our hope!
>    To thee do we cry, poor banished children of Eve.
>    To thee do we send up our sighs,
>     mourning and weeping in this valley of tears!
>    Turn, then, most gracious Advocate,
>     thine eyes of mercy toward us,
>    and after this, our exile,
>   show unto us the blessed fruit of thy womb, Jesus.

O clement, O loving,
O sweet Virgin Mary.

Pray for us, O holy Mother of God - That we may be made worthy
of the promises of Christ.

Let us pray: O God, whose Only Begotten Son, by his life, Death, and
Resurrection, has purchased for us the rewards of eternal life, grant, we
beseech Thee, that meditating on these mysteries of the most holy Rosary of
the Blessed Virgin Mary, we may both imitate what they contain and obtain
what they promise, through the same Christ our Lord. Amen.

The rosary concludes with the Sign of the Cross.

## WAYS OF PRAYING THE ROSARY WITH THIS BOOK

As the next parts of this book will demonstrate, both the traditional mysteries of the
rosary, and the new Romero mysteries, lend themselves to a more meditative,
unrushed prayer, using the message from the Scriptures, words from St Oscar
Romero, reflection questions and prayer.

These materials can accompany private praying of the rosary, or praying the rosary
with a group. Some might just want to pray one of the particular mysteries. As with
the traditional mysteries of joy, light, sorrow, and glory, we can also pray the Romero
mysteries in the more common way of simply announcing the themes for each decade.

Please use this resource in whatever way helps you to pray the rosary, united
spiritually with Our Lady and St Oscar Romero. As you ponder the mysteries of our
faith, come closer to the Lord Jesus who leads us to the Father in the Holy Spirit.

# The Mysteries of the Rosary

## Joy, Light, Sorrow, Glory,

# THE MYSTERIES OF JOY

# The First Mystery of Joy -

# *The Annunciation to Mary of the Birth of the Lord Jesus*

The Message of the Scriptures - St Luke 1:26-38

The Archangel Gabriel, sent by God, announces to the Blessed Virgin Mary that she is to conceive a child in her womb by the overshadowing of the Holy Spirit. She is to call her child Jesus. He 'will be great and will be called the Son of the Most High.' (Lk 1:32) Although troubled by Gabriel's greeting, Mary is reassured not to be afraid, because she has found favour with God. This is the unfolding of God's plan for her life and she trusts in God's promise. 'Behold, I am the servant of the Lord,' said Mary, 'let it be done to me according to your word.' (Lk 1:38)

From the Words of St Oscar Romero

"Do you want to see an act of faith pleasing to the eyes of God? Behold Mary when God seeks her consent to collaborate in our redemption: 'Behold, I am the handmaid of the Lord. May it be done to me according to your word.' (Lk 1:38) This is an act of faith, an acceptance of the mystery of God without understanding it. But it is an acceptance of the One who is all-powerful and knows everything. I don't understand it but I accept it. In God's hands, I am an insignificant instrument. I do not understand the mystery of history, nor do I understand why injustice occurs or why God allows greater injustices for the sake of punishing lesser injustices. I don't understand these things, but I do understand that God is the Lord of history and that I surrender myself to God." (Homily, 2 October 1977)

"Mary is a mother who is blessed for she engages all that is human and embraces all the needs of humanity. When Mary received the angel's message and assented to be the mother of the Saviour, she made herself responsible for all humankind. That fiat, 'May it be done to me according to your word,' (Lk 1:38) is not pronounced only by that young girl of Nazareth; it is the anguished cry of all the peoples who need redemption. We could even say that this crisis of frightening disarray that El Salvador is experiencing in 1979 was already present with all its anguish on the trembling lips of Mary: 'Behold the handmaid. Come to save this people. El Salvador needs you. History needs you. The nations need you. Come!' Mary, then, is the one who gives birth to the mysterious being whom God has promised as a sign of his omnipotence, as a sign of his salvation." (Homily, 23 December 1979)

## REFLECTION QUESTIONS

- Thinking about this mystery, what strikes you in light of the message of Scripture and the words of St Oscar Romero?

- Is there any particular intention, or intentions, for which you would like to pray during this decade of the rosary?

- Carry these thoughts and prayers with you as you pray the Our Father, the ten Hail Marys, and the Glory be.

## PRAYER

At the end of this decade, you might wish to pray:

Heavenly Father,
you brought the Good News of salvation to the world
through Gabriel's message to Mary, our Mother.
In our fear and anxiety,
when the future is unknown or uncertain,
help us to trust your will for us
and increase within us the gifts of faithfulness and hope.
We ask this through Christ Our Lord. Amen.

Holy Mary, Mother of God – Pray for us
St Oscar Romero – Pray for us

# The Second Mystery of Joy-

# The Visitation of Mary to her Cousin Elizabeth

The Message of the Scriptures - St Luke 1:39-56

Pregnant with the unborn Lord Jesus, Our Lady sets out to visit her cousin Elizabeth. Although Elizabeth and Zechariah could not have children, Elizabeth now also carries a child, St John the Baptist, in her womb. When the two women meet, St John the Baptist leaps in Elizabeth's womb. In different ways, God had done the impossible, both for Our Lady and for Elizabeth. Mary is called by Elizabeth 'the mother of my Lord,' (Lk 1:43) acknowledging the divine Son that Our Lady will bring to birth. In the context of this powerful encounter, Mary sings her song of joy and praise, the Magnificat, which begins: 'My soul magnifies the Lord, and my spirit rejoices in God my Saviour.' (Lk 1:46-47)

"When the Virgin proclaims in her marvellous song, the Magnificat, 'The hungry he has filled with good things; the rich he has sent away empty,' (Luke 1:53) what does she mean? It's not that the Virgin despises the rich, but she criticises the self-sufficient and the proud, those who have no need of God, those who make idols of the things of earth. They trust in their money more than in God; they love their wealth more than they love their neighbour. They trust in their power because today they have arms. They abuse others and are proud. These are the ones God sends away empty. But there are those who are humble even if they have power and money; they do not place their hope in these things because they know they are as fleeting as the wind. People will never find stability in power - it comes and goes. True humility consists of trusting in God for everything. If I have power on earth, I must recognise that it comes to me from God, and therefore I must use it as God wants it to be used." (Homily, 28 August 1977)

"Mary challenges us ... to see who is happier: she who is full of grace or the sinner who enjoys the world, but sinfully abuses the things of earth. Mary full of grace is the one who is supremely happy. There is no happiness greater than that of Mary who experiences herself filled with God. That is why we hear ... that hymn with which Mary greets her cousin Saint Elizabeth. As a poet and prophetess praising God, Mary sings her beautiful hymn: 'My soul glorifies the Lord, and I am filled with the joy of God my Saviour because my soul is filled with the almighty One. My soul is filled with a heavenly perfume that cannot be compared to any perfume on earth.' (Lk 1:46- 49)" (Homily, 8 December 1977)

## QUESTIONS FOR REFLECTION

- Thinking about this mystery, what strikes you in light of the message of Scripture and the words of St Oscar Romero?
- Is there any particular intention, or intentions, for which you would like to pray during this decade of the rosary?
- Carry these thoughts and prayers with you as you pray the Our Father, the ten Hail Marys, and the Glory be.

## PRAYER

At the end of this decade, you might wish to pray:

Heavenly Father,
in your Son
you have done great things for us.
Help us to sing your praises with our Mother Mary,
and to play our part in raising up the downtrodden,
supporting those treated unjustly,
and feeding the hungry in our midst.
We ask this through Christ Our Lord. Amen.

Holy Mary, Mother of God – Pray for us
St Oscar Romero – Pray for us

# The Third Mystery of Joy-

## *The Birth of the Lord Jesus in Bethlehem*

The Message of the Scriptures - St Luke 2:1-20

Joseph and Mary, who is pregnant with the unborn Lord Jesus, travel to Bethlehem to register in the census. While there, Mary gives birth to her child, the Son of God 'her firstborn son and wrapped him in swaddling cloths and laid him in a manger, because there was no place for them in the inn.' (Lk 2:7) Angels bring news of Christ's birth to poor sheepherders in the fields. The shepherds come to the manger and find everything as the angels have said. They give glory and praise to God for all they have seen and heard.

From the Words of St Oscar Romero

"Christ is being born today in our people and in our hearts to the degree that every Christian tries to live with integrity the Gospel, the Christian life, the standards of the true Church of God. To the extent that we do this, we are like the apostle and like Mary; we are like the shepherds who give glory to God and sing with joy because they have come to know Christ; and like those humble shepherds of Bethlehem, we try to bring this news to others. To do this, a sincere conversion to Christ is necessary; we must be converted to the love that has visited us; we must echo the infinite goodness of God who brings us redemption. Let us not reject redemption! Let us not be darkness! Let our hearts be open like a cradle so that Christ can be born in each soul tonight and from there flood every heart with light. Then we will sing with the angels the news that we must bring to all people, to the whole of society, and to the whole of the nation: 'Today a Saviour has been born to you!' (Lk 2:11)" (Homily, 24 December 1977)

"If we want to find the child Jesus today, we shouldn't contemplate the lovely figures in our nativity scenes. We should look for him among the malnourished children who went to bed tonight without anything to eat. We should look for him among the poor newspaper boys who will sleep tonight on doorsteps, wrapped in their papers. We should look for him among the poor shoeshine boys who perhaps have earned enough to buy a little gift for their mothers. Or who knows, maybe some of those boys failed to sell all their papers and will be given a tremendous scolding by their stepfather or stepmother. How sad is the situation of our children! All this Jesus takes on himself this very night. Or think of the young campesino [a farm worker] or worker who has no job or suffers some infirmity. Not all is joy tonight. There is much suffering. There are many broken homes. There is much pain and poverty. ... Let us remember the child who was born in a manger and wrapped in cloth so that our poverty, our pain, and our suffering would make sense to us. Let us remember the child whose crib reminds all of us that our destiny is the glory of God in the highest heavens." (Homily, 24 December 1979)

## QUESTIONS FOR REFLECTION

- Thinking about this mystery, what strikes you in light of the message of Scripture and the words of St Oscar Romero?
- Is there any particular intention, or intentions, for which you would like to pray during this decade of the rosary?
- Carry these thoughts and prayers with you as you pray the Our Father, the ten Hail Marys, and the Glory be.

## PRAYER

At the end of this decade, you might wish to pray:

Heavenly Father,
your beloved Son was born in Bethlehem as our Saviour.
He is forever Emmanuel, God-with-us.
Help us to remember he is present to us, and with us, at every moment of our lives, in all the joys and all the sufferings of our world.
May we be Christ's loving presence to others in need.
We ask this through Christ Our Lord. Amen

Holy Mary, Mother of God – Pray for us
St Oscar Romero – Pray for us

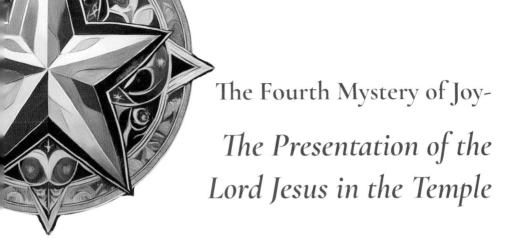

# The Fourth Mystery of Joy-

## *The Presentation of the Lord Jesus in the Temple*

The Message of the Scriptures - St Luke 2:22-38

In accordance with the Law of Moses, Joseph and Mary bring the infant Lord Jesus to the Temple to present him to God and make the prescribed offering of 'a pair of turtledoves, or two young pigeons.' (Lk 2:24) A devout man, Simeon, recognises the Lord Jesus as the 'light for revelation to the Gentiles' and the glory of the people of Israel. (Lk 2:25-32) A prophetess, Anna, also recognises the Lord Jesus 'giving thanks to God' and speaking about him 'to all who were waiting for the redemption of Jerusalem.' (Lk 2:36-38)

## From the Words of St Oscar Romero

"Simeon was awaiting the consolation of Israel and knew that he wasn't going to die before seeing Christ. When he finally saw him, he took him in his hands and pronounced that beautiful prophecy, as if he were a sentinel on watch. ... Here Simeon appears as a watchman, tired after the long night. As he prepares to depart from life, he prays, 'Lord, now you can dismiss your servant in peace for my eyes have seen the salvation of Israel. This child is the light of the nations and the salvation of all peoples.' (Lk 2:29-32) Then, turning to Joseph and Mary, he tells them, 'This child is a sign of contradiction. Good people and bad people who repent will find in him mercy and will receive pardon. But many will also be lost because their selfishness, sinfulness, and pride will make them reject him.' (Lk 2:34) Christ is a stumbling block! That's why I feel a tremendous honour is done me when people reject me, because then I appear a bit more like Jesus Christ who also was a stumbling block." (Homily, 31 December 1978)

"Anna, the venerable octogenarian, was also there, so you can see: persons of all ages are good for announcing Christ! There was Anna, declaring the presence of the Messiah to all who were looking for the liberation of Israel. (Lk 2:36-38) I can just see her now, emerging from the cathedral, that little old lady who saw Christ entering in the arms of the Virgin. She is telling everybody she sees, 'The Redeemer has finally come!', and all those who hear her are filled with joy. How I wish that we were all prophets in this sense of announcing the Lord's coming!" (Homily, 31 December 1978)

## QUESTIONS FOR REFLECTION

- Thinking about this mystery, what strikes you in light of the message of Scripture and the words of St Oscar Romero?
- Is there any particular intention, or intentions, for which you would like to pray during this decade of the rosary?
- Carry these thoughts and prayers with you as you pray the Our Father, the ten Hail Marys, and the Glory be.

## PRAYER

At the end of this decade, you might wish to pray:

Heavenly Father,
like Mary and Joseph, and Simeon and Anna,
may we recognise more fully your Son, Jesus Christ,
as the light of the world and the light of our lives.
Through our words and actions,
help us to share his Gospel message of hope
with everyone we meet,
especially people who are marginalised and ignored.
We ask this through Christ Our Lord. Amen.

Holy Mary, Mother of God – Pray for us
St Oscar Romero – Pray for us

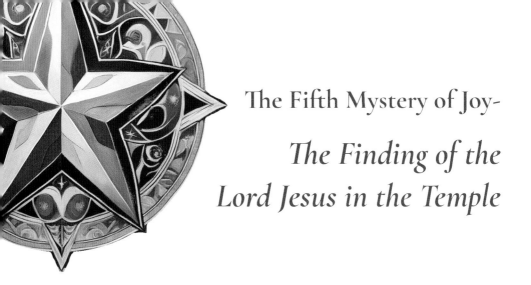

# The Fifth Mystery of Joy-

# *The Finding of the Lord Jesus in the Temple*

The Message of the Scriptures - St Luke 2:41-52

Mary, Joseph, and the twelve-year-old Lord Jesus, travel to Jerusalem for the Feast of the Passover. On the way home, his parents realise Jesus is missing. Unable to find him with their group, they return to the city and search everywhere. Eventually, they find Jesus in the temple, with the teachers, engaging them with conversation and questions. When asked about his absence, Jesus replies, 'Did you not know that I must be in my Father's House?' (Lk 2:49) He returns with them to Nazareth. His mother Mary 'treasured all these things in her heart,' (Lk 2:52) and the Lord Jesus continued to grow in wisdom, advancing in years, and finding favour with God and humanity.

From the Words of St Oscar Romero

"The point of the dialogue between Christ and his parents is to explain to them that there is a heavenly Father who is above earthly mothers and fathers and that young people should not be manipulated by either their fathers or their mothers when there is question of the will of their Father in heaven. The Virgin asked Jesus, 'Son, why have you done this?' And Christ responded with all the tenderness of a human son but also with the courage of a Son of God: 'Why were you looking for me? Did you not know that I had to see about my Father's business?' (Lk 2:48-49) All of us have to say the same thing. … Finally they returned to their home in Nazareth. Soon after Paul VI was elected pontiff, he went to the Holy Land to visit that little house in Nazareth where now a magnificent Church has been built. He remarked at the time, 'Who wouldn't want to live here in the company of that holy family of Nazareth and learn about the simplicity of their life in silence, work, and prayer!' Who wouldn't want our own little houses, dear youth, dear sisters and brothers, no matter how humble they are, to be like that little house of Nazareth!" (Homily, 30 December 1979)

"Wherever Jesus is, there is Mary. The first thing about Mary's presence is that we will never find Mary separated from Jesus or Jesus separated from Mary. Wanting a Christianity without Mary is like separating a precious stone from its ring or a pearl from the gold in which it is mounted. Wanting a Christ without Mary is like wanting a child without the arms of his mother. A Christmas without Mary is meaningless, and so is the dead man abandoned at the foot of the cross, without the affectionate maternal arms that take him down from the cross. Mary is neither divine nor a goddess nor a redeemer, but she is indispensable. She works in such intimate collaboration with God that we cannot do without her." (Homily, 20 January 1980)

## QUESTIONS FOR REFLECTION

- Thinking about this mystery, what strikes you in light of the message of Scripture and the words of St Oscar Romero?

- Is there a particular intention, or intentions, for which you would like to pray during this decade of the rosary?

- Carry these thoughts and prayers with you as you pray the Our Father, the ten Hail Marys, and the Glory be.

## PRAYER

At the end of this decade, you might wish to pray:

Heavenly Father,
we look to the Holy Family of Nazareth
as an example of how to live with love, honour, and respect
in all our relationships.
Help us to imitate the loving witness
of our Mother Mary and St Joseph,
and to play our part in supporting family life,
especially where there is poverty or brokenness.
We ask this through Christ Our Lord. Amen.

Holy Mary, Mother of God – Pray for us
St Oscar Romero – Pray for us

# The Mysteries of Light

# The First Mystery of Light-

## The Baptism of the Lord Jesus in the River Jordan

The Message of the Scriptures - St Matthew 3:13-17

The Lord Jesus approaches St John the Baptist for baptism. At first, John is hesitant, insisting, instead, that he, John, should be baptised by Jesus, not the other way around. However, Jesus says to John 'Let it be so for now, for thus it is fitting for us to fulfil all righteousness.' (Mt 3:15) When Jesus is baptised, the heavens open, the Spirit of God descends like a dove, and a voice from heaven says, 'This is my beloved Son, with whom I am well pleased.' (Mt 3:17)

From the Words of St Oscar Romero

"The God of our Lord Jesus Christ is not a solitary, remote God. ... Christ came to tell us that he is the Son of a Father and that after his death and resurrection the Father would send us a Holy Spirit who would teach us the truth and strengthen this Church. (Jn 14:26) This is truly a great revelation. God is not a solitary being; God is three; God is family; God is communion; God is love shared among three Persons: Father, Son, and Holy Spirit. When John the Baptist baptises Christ there at the Jordan, the gospel tells us about this grand revelation of the Father's voice: 'This is my beloved Son.' (Mt 3:17) Then the presence of the Holy Spirit, exhaled by the love of the Father and the Son, appears as a white dove that rests upon the head of the divine baptised Jesus. (Mt 3:16)" (Homily, 21 May 1978)

"Christ went down to the Jordan River to be baptised among the sinners. This presented a problem for the first Christian communities: explaining why Christ was baptised if he was not a sinner. ... Theology, though, gives us a wonderful solution. Jesus did not need to be baptised. His baptism was not for the purpose of receiving something, as is the case with us when we are baptised. His baptism was not an expression of repentance in order to receive pardon because he didn't need to be pardoned; he was supremely holy. So what was his baptism? ... Christ was baptised not to become the Son of God, but to reveal himself as the Son of God. Christ was not baptised because of any need of his own, but because of our need for him to reveal himself and make himself known." (Homily, 13 January 1980)

## QUESTIONS FOR REFLECTION

- Thinking about this mystery, what strikes you in light of the message of Scripture and the words of St Oscar Romero?
- Is there a particular intention, or intentions, for which you would like to pray during this decade of the rosary?
- Carry these thoughts and prayers with you as you pray the Our Father, the ten Hail Marys, and the Glory be.

## PRAYER

At the end of this decade, you might wish to pray:

Heavenly Father,
at his baptism in the River Jordan,
you called your Son 'the beloved.'
Help us too, to know ourselves to be
your beloved sons and daughters.
Give us hearts and minds also to see
every other person as a beloved
sister or brother, created in your
image and likeness.
We ask this through Christ Our Lord. Amen.

Holy Mary, Mother of God – Pray for us
St Oscar Romero – Pray for us

# The Second Mystery of Light -

## The Miracle at the Wedding Feast at Cana

The Message of the Scriptures - St John 2:1-11

The Lord Jesus and his Blessed Mother, Mary, attend a wedding at Cana in Galilee. At a certain point the wine runs out, a cause of great embarrassment to the host. Our Lady tells Jesus 'They have no wine.' (Jn 2:3) Jesus replies 'Woman, what does this have to do with me? My hour has not come.' (Jn 2:4) However, Mary tells the servant 'Do whatever he tells you.' (Jn 2:5) Jesus asks the servants to fill six enormous stone jars full of water. When the wedding steward drinks from them, the water has now changed into the best wine, kept until last. St John says this is the first of the signs Jesus worked, where he 'manifested his glory.' (Jn 2:11)

## From the Words of St Oscar Romero

"'Woman, my hour has not yet come.' (Jn 2:4) The 'hour' of Christ expressed something very close to his heart. His hour would come when, nailed to the cross, he redeemed the world and when, risen, he was glorified by God. The pain was not separated from the glory: cross and paschal mystery are the sign, they are the hour. That hour had not yet arrived, chronologically speaking, when Mary made her request. But in essence what he told her was this: 'What I am going to do now is something that foreshadows my hour. I am going to give a glimpse of the glorification that will be consummated on the day when I die on the cross and am raised up. Even now my miracles will explain the meaning of that death and that resurrection. After my glorification, mother, you who have collaborated in this redemption will have a very active, fruitful part to play. We will anticipate that hour now, but only then will you completely assume your role of motherly intercession in the history of humankind.'" (Homily, 20 January 1980)

"Our attitude as the Church should be like that of Mary: both trusting and active. We should pray as though everything depended on God and work as though everything depended on us. Indeed, no sooner had Mary made her request of Jesus than she told the servants, 'Let us do our part. Let us fill the water jars, and let us do what he says.' (Jn 2:5) A miracle can't happen when people are only waiting for God to act. We have to do all that we're capable of doing. The miracle happens, but not without our doing something. Mary is the most marvellous combination of faith and action, and that is what every Catholic should be as well: a marvellous combination both of human values and of faith that trusts completely in God. We need to believe in our human action and place our confidence in human beings." (Homily, 20 January 1980)

## QUESTIONS FOR REFLECTION

- Thinking about this mystery, what strikes you in light of the message of Scripture and the words of St Oscar Romero?
- Is there a particular intention, or intentions, for which you would like to pray during this decade of the rosary?
- Carry these thoughts and prayers with you as you pray the Our Father, the ten Hail Marys, and the Glory be.

## PRAYER

At the end of this decade, you might wish to pray:

Heavenly Father,
the Lord Jesus, prompted by his Mother,
gave a sign of the new life to come from his
cross and resurrection when he changed water into wine.
This was also a sign of your kingdom among us,
where injustice is to be changed to justice,
where hatred is to be changed into peace,
where enemies are to be changed into friends.
Help us to be more like Christ so that
we can play our part in bringing your kingdom to life.
We ask this through Christ Our Lord. Amen.

Holy Mary, Mother of God – Pray for us
St Oscar Romero – Pray for us

# The Third Mystery of Light -

# The Proclamation of the Kingdom of God and the Call to Conversion

The Message of the Scriptures - St Mark 1:14-15

After his baptism in the River Jordan, and his temptation in the desert, the Lord Jesus enters Galilee. There he declares the Good News of God, saying 'The time is fulfilled, and the kingdom of God is at hand; repent and believe in the Gospel.' (Mk 1:15) His proclamation of the kingdom and his call to conversion go hand in hand.

From the Words of St Oscar Romero

"Christ teaches us that his incarnation is precisely that message and that preaching synthesised by Mark in this succinct phrase: 'This is the time of fulfilment. The kingdom of God is at hand. Repent and believe in the Gospel.' (Mk 1:15) Be converted to the Good News! The Good News that Jesus brought was the announcement of great hope, the formation of a humanity where all would be sisters and brothers to one another and God would be seen as Father of all. In our effort to come to know the true God we will recognise that every sister and brother is the image of God, and in our effort to love one another and avoid being divided into social classes by hatred and vengeance, we will draw near to God." (Homily, 6 August 1977)

"'The kingdom of God has arrived! Be converted and believe in the Good News!' (Mk 1:15) This is the foundation of God's kingdom. Conversion is the same as doing penance. It is the same as the famous Greek word *metanoia*, which means being converted, changing one's mentality. Those who had bowed down before the idols of earth now had to change their mentality and kneel down instead before the only Lord. Being converted means returning to God, and since the way back to God is by Jesus Christ - who said 'I am the way: no one comes to the Father except through me' (Jn 14:6) - conversion means clinging to Christ and seeking the Father." (Homily, 9 March 1980)

## QUESTIONS FOR REFLECTION

- Thinking about this mystery, what strikes you in light of the message of Scripture and the words of St Oscar Romero?
- Is there a particular intention, or intentions, for which you would like to pray during this decade of the rosary?
- Carry these thoughts and prayers with you as you pray the Our Father, the ten Hail Marys, and the Glory be.

## PRAYER

At the end of this decade, you might wish to pray:

Heavenly Father,
open our hearts and minds to hear again
your Son's call to repentance and conversion.
Remove our blindness to injustice and violence.
Give us ears to hear the cry of the earth
and the cry of the poor.
In the power of the Holy Spirit,
help us to be witnesses who put our faith into action.
We ask this through Christ Our Lord. Amen.

Holy Mary, Mother of God – Pray for us
St Oscar Romero – Pray for us

# The Fourth Mystery of Light –

## The Transfiguration of the Lord

The Message of the Scriptures – St Matthew 17:1-9

The Lord Jesus leads Peter, James, and John, up a high mountain. In their presence, he is transfigured. His face shines like the sun and his clothes become white as light. Moses and Elijah appear with him. A cloud overshadows them and a voice speaks from the cloud, 'This is my beloved Son, with whom I am well pleased; listen to him.' (Mt 17:5) The disciples fall down in terror, but Jesus touches them and tells them not to be afraid. Then they see only Jesus again and he leads them down the mountain, telling them not to say anything about what they had experienced 'until the Son of Man is raised from the dead.' (Mt 17:9)

"On this morning of the transfiguration, sisters and brothers, it's interesting to observe the persons who surround Christ. (Mt 17:1,3) They are all violent persons: Moses killed an Egyptian when he saw his people oppressed in Egypt. (Ex 2:11-12) Elijah slaughtered the false prophets who impugned the dignity of the true God. (1 Kgs 18:40) Peter drew his sword when they assaulted Christ in the darkness of Gethsemane. (Jn 18:10) James and John were called by Christ himself ... 'the sons of thunder,' because they were impetuous men; one day they wanted to rain fire down on a town that didn't want to receive Jesus and his disciples. (Mk 3:17; Lk 9:54) We see these men there with all their potential for violence and all their aggressive force, but they are docile before Christ. Aggressiveness is an instinct that God has given us, but some people don't know how to use it rightly. Christ told James and John, 'You do not know of what spirit you are. The Son of Man has not come to kill but to save.' (Lk 9:55-56) Christ does not mutilate our human powers, but orients them by Christian power." (Homily, 6 August 1978)

"Standing on the heights of Tabor, Christ is a magnificent image of liberation. That's how God wants us to be: freed from sin and death and hell, and living his eternal, immortal, glorious life. This is our destiny. Talking about heaven is not something alienating; it motivates us to undertake our great responsibilities on earth more seriously and more passionately. Nobody does the earthly work of seeking the people's political liberation with more enthusiasm than those who hope that all the liberation struggles of history will be incorporated into the great victory of Christ's liberation. For as the [Second Vatican] Council says, we know that everything that we promote in the world - justice, peace, loving words, appeals to sanity - we will later find transfigured in the beauty of our eternal reward. Christ, therefore, is the model of God's plan of liberation." (Homily, 2 March 1980)

## QUESTIONS FOR REFLECTION

- Thinking about this mystery, what strikes you in light of the message of Scripture and the words of St Oscar Romero?
- Is there a particular intention, or intentions, for which you would like to pray during this decade of the rosary?
- Carry these thoughts and prayers with you as you pray the Our Father, the ten Hail Marys, and the Glory be.

## PRAYER

At the end of this decade, you might wish to pray:

Heavenly Father,
like Peter, James, and John,
we can struggle to understand the meaning
of your Son's death and resurrection.
Help us to look to the Lord Jesus
and to seek our transfiguration,
and that of our world, through union with him
and our commitment to working for change for the better.
We ask this through Christ Our Lord. Amen.

Holy Mary, Mother of God – Pray for us
St Oscar Romero – Pray for us

# The Fifth Mystery of Light -

# The Institution of the Holy Eucharist

The Message of the Scriptures - St Luke 22:14-20

The night before the Lord Jesus dies on the cross, he gathers his disciples in the Upper Room to celebrate the Passover. During the meal, he takes some bread, gives thanks, breaks it and gives it to them saying, 'This is my body, which is given for you. Do this in remembrance of me.' (Lk 22:19) Then, in a similar way, he takes a cup of wine, and says, 'This cup that is poured out for you is the new covenant in my blood.' (Lk 22:20)

From the Words of St Oscar Romero

"The Body and the Blood of the Lord, present on the altar each time that a priest celebrates Mass, become the same sacrifice of Christ on the cross; the whole history of Israel culminates there on the altar. Moreover, as Saint Paul just told us, in the Eucharist 'we proclaim the death of the Lord until he comes.' (1 Cor 11:26) The Christian people are a people who live with a memory, the memory of Calvary. But it is not just a memory; it is something present and even becomes hope for the future. This Christ who becomes present in our host at the Mass is the Christ who will return; he is the Christ who will come to judge history; he is the Christ in whom all peoples find the solution to their problems. The definitive solution can be found only in him because he is the hope of the people who travel through history as tormented martyrs, always hoping for the definitive liberation that is to come." (Homily, 23 March 1978)

"When the priest says the words we heard in today's gospel, 'Take and eat, this is my body. This is my blood of the Christian covenant which is shed for the forgiveness of sins,' (Mk 14:22,24) and lifts the host high, then the people - whether standing as a sign of respect or kneeling as a sign of adoration - acknowledge that before their eyes, in the sign of bread and wine, the Body and the Blood of the Lord are truly, really, and substantially present. This is a living presence that gives life. The presence of Christ in the Eucharist has two aspects. First, he is present as victim, as sacrifice; the sacrifice of Christ on the cross becomes wholly real in every Mass that is celebrated. Second, he is present as communion, by which Christ nourishes us with love. ... He is the victim who gathers together the sacrifices of all men and women to offer them to God. And he is also communion, calling everyone to form a single family in love, the family of God which is nourished with the Flesh and the Blood of the heavenly Lamb, the bread that descends from heaven." (Homily, 17 June 1979)

## QUESTIONS FOR REFLECTION

- Thinking about this mystery, what strikes you in light of the message of Scripture and the words of St Oscar Romero?
- Is there a particular intention, or intentions, for which you would like to pray during this decade of the rosary?
- Carry these thoughts and prayers with you as you pray the Our Father, the ten Hail Marys, and the Glory be.

## PRAYER

At the end of this decade, you might wish to pray:

Heavenly Father,
thank you for the gift of the Eucharist in your Church.
As the Lord Jesus gives himself to us,
in his body and his blood,
may we give ourselves to you.
May we be willing to make sacrifices, however small,
so that others in need, at home and abroad,
can live with dignity and hope.
We ask this through Christ Our Lord. Amen.

Holy Mary, Mother of God – Pray for us
St Oscar Romero – Pray for us

# The Mysteries of Sorrow

# The First Mystery of Sorrow -

# *The Agony of the Lord Jesus in the Garden of Gethsemane*

The Message of the Scriptures - St Luke 22:40-46

The Lord Jesus takes his disciples to the Garden of Gethsemane, asking them to pray that they might not 'enter into temptation.' (Lk 22:40) He moves a short distance away to pray in solitude, asking the Father, 'If you are willing, remove this cup from me. Nevertheless, not my will, but yours be done.' (Lk 22:42) An angel appears to strengthen Jesus, and his sweat falls like drops of blood. When Jesus returns from prayer, he finds the disciples asleep. 'Why are you sleeping?' he says to them, 'Rise and pray that you may not enter into temptation.' (Lk 22:46)

From the Words of St Oscar Romero

"Christ exclaims, 'Now my soul is troubled, and what shall I say? "Father, save me from this hour?" But it was for this purpose that I came to this hour!' (Jn 12:27) See how strong the instinct of self-preservation is! Christ was not an unfeeling being. Christ was a man of flesh and blood, nerves and muscles, just like us. ... We are anticipating the night in Gethsemane. In our Christian reflection today, let us not forget the figure of Christ, his face bathed in tears as he cried out to the one who could save him. (Heb 5:7) He cried out as one overwhelmed by what was coming upon him, 'My soul is troubled. Father, save me from this hour!' But his final disposition is that of obedience: 'But it is for this that I have come to this hour.' (Jn 12:27) This is what is beautiful about Christ's sacrifice: he gave himself over freely in obedience to the Father." (Homily, 1 April 1979)

"Everything Christ went through would have been of no use at all if he were not motivated by obedience. The essence of Christ's passion was his obedient surrender to the Father. He offered himself with a sense of making reparation: 'Father, if those lashes are necessary for you to forgive all the sins of the world, then let them fall on me. If the crown of thorns must be woven so as to pierce my temples, then let it cleave to my head so that you will forgive all my sisters and brothers. If there is need for the horror of having my muscles pierced with nails and my side opened by a spear, then let it be, Lord, because that means the redemption of my sisters and brothers.' This is what is most beautiful and attractive in Christ: he took the place of sinners like me. I should have suffered, I should have been punished, I should have been thrown into hell, forever estranged from the Father. But Christ wanted to bear the fullness of my guilt so that I might find reconciliation. And now that same obedience with which Christ paid for all my disobedience is mine!" (Homily,1 April 1979)

## QUESTIONS FOR REFLECTION

- Thinking about this mystery, what strikes you in light of the message of Scripture and the words of St Oscar Romero?
- Is there a particular intention, or intentions, for which you would like to pray during this decade of the rosary?
- Carry these thoughts and prayers with you as you pray the Our Father, the ten Hail Marys, and the Glory be.

## PRAYER

At the end of this decade, you might wish to pray:

Heavenly Father,
in the Garden of Gethsemane,
your Son experienced the challenge of suffering and obedience.
Help us, like him,
always to seek, not our own will,
but your holy will for our lives.
Keep us faithful to what is true, right and just,
especially when faced with the temptation
to remain silent and inactive in the face of injustice.
We ask this through Christ Our Lord. Amen.

Holy Mary, Mother of God – Pray for us
St Oscar Romero – Pray for us

# The Second Mystery of Sorrow -

# *The Scourging of the Lord Jesus at the Pillar*

The Message of the Scriptures - St Mark 15:6-15

The Lord Jesus is brought before the Roman Governor, Pontius Pilate. According to a custom of releasing a criminal at Passover, he asks the crowd whether they want him to release the murderer Barabbas or Jesus. The crowd asks for Barabbas and cry for Jesus to be crucified. 'So Pilate, wishing to satisfy the crowd, released for them Barabbas, and having scourged Jesus, he delivered him to be crucified.' (Mk 15:15)

"Christ had to drink from the bitter cup of the passion. When Peter took out his sword to defend him, he was told, 'Put your sword back in its sheath because those who kill by the sword will perish by the sword.' (Jn 18:10-11) It was necessary to carry the cross and be condemned to death as a vile criminal. Nothing mattered except what the Father wanted. It was the Father's will that the sin of the world be washed away with the blood of Jesus, the Son of God, because it was so awful. When we feel rebellious, let us reflect that the truest rebellion is the holy rebelliousness of God, for he does not submit to our human sin but asks us to be purified. It was necessary to ask for the blood of his own Son and not to pardon him, so that all our iniquities could be loaded onto his back." (Homily, 23 September 1979)

"The wicked say, 'He says he is a son of God! Let us test him and see if God saves him!' (Wis 2:16-20) Poor things! They think everything is resolved in this temporal history. They think that by humiliating Christians with torture and imprisonment they are triumphing, but they have no idea. When speaking of the martyrs, Saint Augustine used to say, 'Do you see the executioner holding his triumphant sword over the body of a martyr? Who has conquered? There is no question but that the victim is the victor!' Those who have conquered by the brute force of the sword have not comprehended the greatness of those who have given their lives for a sublime ideal. This is the true victory that overcomes the world. ... We are living in a dark night, but Christians can discern beyond the night the glow of dawn, and they carry in their hearts the hope that never fails. Christ walks by our side! Let us not fear! We are children of God even though some laugh at this title, just as they laughed at Christ: 'He says he is the Son of God! Let God save him!' (Mt 27:43) They mocked him, thinking that they had triumphed over the Son of God. Christ could have

come down from the cross and annihilated his enemies, reducing them to dust, but he kept all his greatness hidden within himself. He was moved by a conviction the blind could not understand: he had to save the world." (Homily, 23 September 1979)

## QUESTIONS FOR REFLECTION

- Thinking about this mystery, what strikes you in light of the message of Scripture and the words of St Oscar Romero?
- Is there a particular intention, or intentions, for which you would like to pray during this decade of the rosary?
- Carry these thoughts and prayers with you as you pray the Our Father, the ten Hail Marys, and the Glory be.

## PRAYER

At the end of this decade, you might wish to pray:

Heavenly Father,
Jesus faced rejection, humiliation, and torture.
He stands in solidarity with everyone today who is mistreated and abused.
Strengthen us to stand beside those in need, and to work for justice.
Help us to believe that in loving the dejected, we are loving your Son.
We ask this through Christ Our Lord. Amen.

Holy Mary, Mother of God – Pray for us
St Oscar Romero – Pray for us

# The Third Mystery of Sorrow -

# *The Crowning of the Lord Jesus with Thorns*

The Message of the Scriptures - St Mark 15:16-20

The Lord Jesus is taken inside the Roman Governor's Palace and the soldiers humiliate and mock him. A purple cloak is wrapped around his shoulders. Some thorny brambles are twisted into a crown which is placed upon his head. As the soldiers pretend to honour Jesus as a king, kneeling before him and saluting him, at the same time they hit him and spit on him.

"Christ was not abandoned, but he certainly felt all the pain and anguish that the human heart must suffer in the course of life. It is the psychological suffering of feeling all alone, completely abandoned, with no one who understands. In his loneliness Christ left us that word of distress to help us in our prayer and devotion and to strengthen our faith in the one true God. God is not failing us when we do not feel his presence. We shouldn't say, 'God doesn't help me with what I earnestly pray for, and so I'll pray no more.' God exists, and the further away he seems to be, the more he exists! When you think that God is far away and doesn't hear you, that is when he is closest to you. When you feel anguish and want God to draw close because you feel his absence, that is when God is very close to your distress. When are we going to understand that God doesn't give us only happiness? He also tests our faithfulness during our moments of distress. Our prayer and our devotion have more merit when we remain faithful even though the Lord seems far away. May this cry of Christ teach us that God is always a Father who never abandons us and that we are closer to him than we think." (Homily, 13 April 1979)

"The representative of the powerful Roman empire asked the bound prisoner, 'Are you the king of the Jews?' (Jn 18:33) Christ ended that dialogue with Pilate by saying, 'Yes, I am a king. For this I was born: to testify to the truth. Everyone who belongs to the truth listens to my voice.' (Jn 18:37) John's narration continues with the crowning with thorns, the mockery of the sceptre, the cloak, the throne, the cross. Yet in the midst of these blood-spattered ceremonies, a king was being enthroned. Through the ironic circumstance of a man condemned to death, God seized the empire of Rome as his instrument and proclaimed the truth of that inscription on the cross: 'Jesus the Nazarene, King of the Jews.' (Jn 19:19) And not only of the Jews, but of all peoples. As we gather

together all the rich content of that trial, we remove his thorns and wipe away his blood, and it becomes wonderfully clear that Christ is a king very different from the kings of this world." (Homily, 25 November 1979)

## QUESTIONS FOR REFLECTION

- Thinking about this mystery, what strikes you in light of the message of Scripture and the words of St Oscar Romero?
- Is there a particular intention, or intentions, for which you would like to pray during this decade of the rosary?
- Carry these thoughts and prayers with you as you pray the Our Father, the ten Hail Marys, and the Glory be.

## PRAYER

At the end of this decade, you might wish to pray:

Heavenly Father, we see your Son mocked and humiliated.
Our hearts break for love of him.
Had we been there, we tell ourselves, we would have defended him;
but things are not always so easy.
Help us, today, to protect and speak on behalf
of those tortured and treated unjustly.
Help us not to be passive or silent in the face of oppression
We ask this through Christ Our Lord. Amen.

Holy Mary, Mother of God – Pray for us
St Oscar Romero – Pray for us

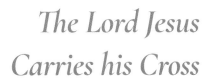

# The Fourth Mystery of Sorrow -

## *The Lord Jesus Carries his Cross*

The Message of the Scriptures - St Luke 23:26-32

As the Lord Jesus carries his cross to Calvary, he is exhausted and falls under its weight. The soldiers force Simon from Cyrene to carry the cross for Jesus. An enormous crowd follows Jesus and lines the route of his way to crucifixion. Jesus says to a group of women who are mourning and lamenting for him, 'Daughters of Jerusalem, do not weep for me, but weep for yourselves and for your children.' (Lk 23:28)

From the Words of St Oscar Romero

> "Jesus was humiliated by undergoing a death that could not be inflicted on Romans because they were free, but it was imposed on people

enslaved. Rome crucified people but not those who were Roman citizens. Romans crucified those who were subject to their empire. Since Palestine was subject to Rome - Pilate was the Roman governor over that oppressed people - Christ had to be debased as a person unworthy of citizenship. He had to die humiliated. The incarnation led him to this extreme, but from that humiliation he began to be exalted. ... 'Because of this, God greatly exalted him and bestowed on him the name that is above every name, that at the name of Jesus every knee should bend, of those in heaven and on earth and under the earth, and every tongue confess that Jesus Christ is Lord.' (Phil 2:9-11) This is the glory of our Redeemer. Let us not forget this as we look upon Jesus humiliated beneath the weight of the cross. ... Let us say from the depth of our faith, 'Though he seems to be like me in my suffering, he is the Lord, and though I seem to be like him in carrying the cross, I will share in his glory.' Jesus does not pass through the painful tunnel of torture and death all alone. Travelling with him is a whole people, and we will also rise with him. We have read the passion, the greatest story about a man who has suffered. There is no one like Christ." (Homily, 19 March 1978)

"It is no wonder, sisters and brothers, that the people, feeling humiliated like Christ, should want to shake off their crosses, break free of the nails and the lashes, and liberate themselves. And so liberators of the people arise, but many in a false sense. ... Listen to this first word of Christ: 'Father, forgive them for they know not what they do.' (Lk 23:34) How far the liberator is from hatred, resentment, and vengeance! He could have unleashed the forces of nature and destroyed those who crucified him. He could have freed himself and pulverised his persecutors, but he wants no violence. One day when John and James resented the ingratitude of the Samaritans who refused them lodging, they asked Jesus to send fire down upon that city. Christ told them, 'You do not know what manner of spirit you are, for the Son of Man came not to destroy lives but to save them and to give his life for the salvation of all.' (Lk 9:54-56; 19:10) This is Christian liberation. Christians in the Church must offer their collaboration in the liberation of our people, but with an attitude of love and forgiveness modelled on Christ's plea: 'Father, forgive them!' (Lk 23:34)" (Homily, 24 March 1978)

## QUESTIONS FOR REFLECTION

- Thinking about this mystery, what strikes you in light of the message of Scripture and the words of St Oscar Romero?
- Is there a particular intention, or intentions, for which you would like to pray during this decade of the rosary?
- Carry these thoughts and prayers with you as you pray the Our Father, the ten Hail Marys, and the Glory be.

## PRAYER

At the end of this decade, you might wish to pray:

> Heavenly Father, we cannot choose the crosses
> we are called to carry during our life.
> Help us to face the cross, in our own life and the lives of others,
> consoled by the presence of Christ.
> Like Simon of Cyrene, help us also to share the burdens of others,
> to stand with them in solidarity and to be a voice for the voiceless.
> We ask this through Christ Our Lord. Amen.
>
> Holy Mary, Mother of God – Pray for us
> St Oscar Romero – Pray for us

# The Fifth Mystery of Sorrow -

# The Crucifixion and Death of the Lord Jesus

The Message of the Scriptures - St Matthew 27:35-61

The Lord Jesus is nailed to the cross beside two criminals. People shout abuse at him: 'You who would destroy the temple and rebuild it in three days, save yourself! If you are the Son of God, come down from the cross.' (Mt 27:40) 'Standing beside his cross is Mary, his mother, and John the beloved disciple.' (Jn 19:26) 'When Jesus saw his Mother and the disciple whom he loved standing nearby, he said to his mother, "Woman, behold your son!" Then he said to the disciple, "Behold, your mother!"' (Jn 19:26-27) At the ninth hour, Jesus cried out with a loud voice and gave up his spirit and died.

From the Words of St Oscar Romero

"'Woman, behold your son! Son, behold your mother.' (Jn 19:26-27) Christ's liberation, sisters and brothers, is tenderness and love; it is the presence of a kind mother, Mary, who is a model for those who collaborate with Christ in liberating earth and gaining heaven. In her hymn of thanksgiving Mary proclaims the greatness of God and declares that God will reject the pride of the powerful and will exalt the humble. (Lk 1:46-55) She teaches us that the road of true liberation and Christian redemption is the road of humility, the road of love, the road of commitment like her own. We are invited to love one another and discover in her the bright road that leads us to Jesus." (Homily, 24 March 1978)

"And so the final word uttered by the Lord was one of confidence as he placed his life and death in the arms of God. From Christ's lips came once again words of filial trust: 'Father, into your hands I commend my spirit!' (Lk 23:46) May we also at the hour of our death experience the presence of the Father accepting our life and our spirit. When we pass on, may we be satisfied that we have left behind on earth a struggle that was inspired in love and faith and hope, not a struggle of blood and violence! How tragic it would be, sisters and brothers, to leave in our wake people who were tortured, disappeared, killed - to leave a trail of terrorism, arson, and crimes. What reckoning before God will have to be given by those bloodstained hands that whipped and beat their sisters and brothers? How sad will it be in that hour not to be able to tell God, 'Father, into your hands I commend my spirit.' (Lk 23:46) How sad it will be at the time of our death if we cannot present to God a spirit that worked on earth with love and hope and faith, but only a spirit involved in bloody struggle that God wants no part of!" (Homily, 24 March 1978)

## QUESTIONS FOR REFLECTION

- Thinking about this mystery, what strikes you in light of the message of Scripture and the words of St Oscar Romero?
- Is there a particular intention, or intentions, for which you would like to pray during this decade of the rosary?
- Carry these thoughts and prayers with you as you pray the Our Father, the ten Hail Marys, and the Glory be.

## PRAYER

At the end of this decade, you might wish to pray:

Heavenly Father,
we stand silent before the
suffering and death of your Son.
Help us to live in such a way
that, when the time of our death approaches,
we can make his prayer our own:
'Father, into your hands I commit my spirit.'
In the face of innocent suffering and death,
inspire us to cry out on behalf of the victims of violence.
We ask this through Christ Our Lord. Amen.

Holy Mary, Mother of God – Pray for us
St Oscar Romero – Pray for us

# The Mysteries of Glory

# The First Mystery of Glory-

# The Resurrection of the Lord Jesus from the Dead

The Message of the Scriptures - St John 20:1-20

Early in the morning, on the third day after the Lord Jesus was crucified, Mary Magdalene goes to the tomb where his body was buried. She sees the stone covering the entrance has been rolled away and she runs to tell the apostles Peter and John. They rush to the tomb and find it empty. The garments in which Jesus' body was wrapped are there, but his body is not. The disciples return home, but Mary remains. The Lord Jesus, raised from the dead, appears to her and calls her by name. Mary goes to announce to the disciples 'I have seen the Lord.' (Jn 20:18) Later that day, Jesus appears to his disciples and says to them, 'Peace be with you.' (Jn 20:19)

From the Words of St Oscar Romero

"Christ transmitted to the Church all his paschal power, that is, all the power of that passage from death to life, with all that those two words imply. ... For death is sin, mediocrity, injustice, turmoil, abuse of human rights, disorder in all human realities – all of this must be buried in the tomb of the Lord and then raised to new life; that is, it must pass from death to life. Life means justice. Life means respect for the human person. Life means holiness; it means every effort to be a little better each day because every man and every woman, every young person and every child, begins to feel that his or her life is a vocation that God has given them to become present in the world. They become present not only in the wonders of creation as images of God, but also in the wonders of redemption which exalt nature, society, and friendship. ... Let us walk with Jesus so that the Easter feast ... might be an invitation to work in a way that makes the world more human and more Christian." (Homily, 17 April 1977)

"As we behold the risen Christ, our faith should overflow with gratitude and delight and hope. We should tell him, 'You are the God who became man and who for love of humankind was not afraid to hide your grandeur as God and pass through this world as a man like any other. So little did you distinguish yourself from others that they associated you with criminals, and you died as an outlaw on the cross on Calvary. They buried you in the garbage dump of those who were crucified, but from there, from the garbage dump, from the depths of the abyss, from the descent into the realms of shadow and death, you now rise up as the divine risen One, truly anointed by God with the power of the Holy Spirit.' (Acts 10:38) ... The Church cannot be deaf or mute, sisters and brothers, before the entreaty of millions of people who are oppressed by a thousand slaveries and are crying out for liberation. But the Church tells them what the true freedom is that they must seek: it is the freedom that Christ introduced to earth when he rose and burst the chains of sin and death and hell. To be like Christ, free of sin, is to be really free with true liberation. Those who put their faith in the risen One and work for a more just world; those who protest against the injustices of the present system, against the abuses of unjust authorities, against the wrongfulness of humans exploiting humans; those who base all these struggles on the resurrection of the great Liberator - these alone are authentic Christians." (Homily, 26 March 1978)

## QUESTIONS FOR REFLECTION

- Thinking about this mystery, what strikes you in light of the message of Scripture and the words of St Oscar Romero?
- Is there a particular intention, or intentions, for which you would like to pray during this decade of the rosary?
- Carry these thoughts and prayers with you as you pray t Our Father, the ten Hail Marys, and the Glory be.

## PRAYER

At the end of this decade, you might wish to pray:

Heavenly Father,
the resurrection of your Son from the dead
has forever transformed our world and our lives.
Deepen our faith in the power of his victory over sin and death.
Help us to live in the strength of his triumph
and to work for the release of those entombed in poverty, injustice, and despair.
We ask this through Christ Our Lord. Amen.

Holy Mary, Mother of God – Pray for us
St Oscar Romero – Pray for us

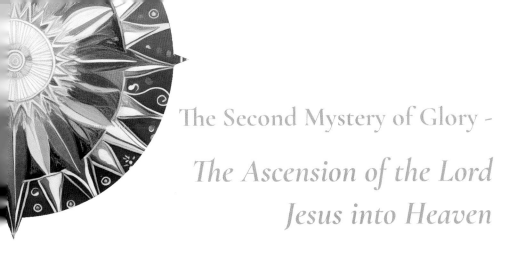

# The Second Mystery of Glory -

# The Ascension of the Lord Jesus into Heaven

The Message of the Scriptures - Acts of the Apostles 1:6-11

After his resurrection, the Lord Jesus gathers with his disciples. He tells them they will receive power when the Holy Spirit comes upon them, and they will be his witnesses, not just in the local towns and districts, but also to the ends of the world. Jesus then ascends on high, until he disappears from the disciples' sight. While they gaze into the air, two angelic figures address them: 'Men of Galilee, why do you stand looking into heaven? This Jesus who was taken up from you into heaven, will come in the same way as you saw him go into heaven.' (Acts 1:6)

From the Words of St Oscar Romero

"Only Christ is the Lord, and the Church's mission is to preach to humankind, especially to those who bow and scrape before the idols of earth, and to tell them that it is not licit to create idols out of the goods of the earth. Only Christ is the Lord. The Church tells her faithful: blessed are you Christians poor in spirit, poor in your detachment, poor in your efforts to create a better world, for you follow the true liberator, Christ the Lord, the one who gives human beings their true dignity. Neither communism nor capitalism adores Christ; they adore their idols. The Church adores her Christ, and on this day proclaims him to be the goal toward which she directs the ideals of all Christians. Christ ascending into heaven is the ideal of true human development, which culminates in identification with God himself." (Homily, 22 May 1977)

"Forty days after being raised, Christ ascends to the Father. ... From the very moment Christ rose, from the time that his physical life is no longer of this earth, he leaves his mystical life breathing over us in his Spirit. Just as the Creator breathed intelligent life into the clay in creation, (Gen 2:7) so Christ on the very day of resurrection breathes his new Spirit, his resurrection, his Passover onto those who would become the Church: 'Receive the Holy Spirit.' (Jn 20:22) Fifty days later, however, on Pentecost, that presence became manifest in the form of a hurricane and in tongues of fire. (Acts 2:2-3) That silent Spirit that always accompanies the Church is hurricane, is fire, is the power that impels the Church. ... Jesus is with us in the stage between heavenly life and earthly life. But he does not leave us orphans, as he told us with these precious words: 'Whoever loves me will keep my word and my Father will love him, and we will come to him and make our dwelling with him. ... I have told you this while I am with you. The Advocate, the Holy Spirit that the Father will send in my name - he will teach you everything and remind you of all that I told you.' (Jn 14:23-26) ... Jesus said, 'Peace I leave with you.' (Jn 14:27) ... This peace cannot be confused with the peace of the world because it is dynamic, it is active, and it flows from faith and hope. It does not remain silent but loves and lives; it is a peace that moves toward that ultimate peace where God is everything for all people." (Homily, 15 May 1977)

## QUESTIONS FOR REFLECTION

- Thinking about this mystery, what strikes you in light of the message of Scripture and the words of St Oscar Romero?
- Is there a particular intention, or intentions, for which you would like to pray during this decade of the rosary?
- Carry these thoughts and prayers with you as you pray the Our Father, the ten Hail Marys, and the Glory be.

## PRAYER

At the end of this decade, you might wish to pray:

Heavenly Father,
your Son ascended back to you
having completed his earthly ministry.
He sends us out into the world
in the power of the Holy Spirit.
Help us to be witnesses to Christ,
to be advocates and agents of his love,
and to make our world a better place by what we say and how we live.
We ask this through Christ Our Lord. Amen.

Holy Mary, Mother of God – Pray for us
St Oscar Romero – Pray for us

# The Third Mystery of Glory -

# The Descent of the Holy Spirit on the Apostles at Pentecost

The Message of the Scriptures - Acts of the Apostles 2:1-13

After his Ascension, Mary, the Mother of the Lord, gathered with the apostles in prayer. (Acts 1:13-14) At Pentecost, fifty days after the resurrection of the Lord Jesus, the disciples gather with each other. A sound comes from heaven, like a mighty wind, filling their house. Then flames of fire rest on the head of each of the apostles, who are filled with the Holy Spirit and begin to speak a new kind of language. Others, from different territories, can understand what they are saying as if it were their own speech.

From the Words of St Oscar Romero

"No one can say, 'Jesus is Lord,' except by the Holy Spirit." (1 Cor 12:3b)
Reflect on this phrase. With our lips we can say, 'Jesus is Lord,' but we can

feel and understand the depth of meaning only if God allows us to speak with him, only if we feel we have the ability to pray. Those who do not pray have not developed their full human potential. Those who do not pray because they do not believe in God are mutilated. Those who do not pray because they kneel down before the god of materialism - be it money or politics or anything else - have not understood the true greatness of being a human person. ... This is Pentecost; this is the Church: bringing this message to humankind. That is why the Church above all proclaims her religious mission and teaches people to pray. She is distressed when her children do not pray as we have so often urged. This is the soul of our Church, sisters and brothers. The Holy Spirit is nothing more than that God who enters into communication with us and invites us to use our freedom and our intelligence in order to open ourselves to the Absolute and enter into dialogue with the One who created us, who made us capable of becoming his children, who awaits us in heaven, who consoles us on earth, and who leads us along paths that are worthy of the children of God." (Homily, 29 May 1977)

"Pentecost, then, is the Church's birthday because on this day the Church was born. The Church is the group of those who believe in Christ and receive the Spirit of Christ; they receive the all-powerful breath of the Messiah and Redeemer in order to make all his people into redeemers and messiahs. All of us, dear Christians, are this new creation. The world cannot be renewed without us, and we are responsible for the renewal of the world. Starting from that day, Christ has set up his kingdom in the midst of humanity so that God's kingdom is now being built up on this earth. Preaching about a Church that hopes only in fulfilment after death falsifies the kingdom of God. The kingdom that Christ preached and established is precisely the one created by his breath; it is the kingdom of concrete individuals on pilgrimage through history who are responsible for transforming history into God's kingdom. ... The Church needs only hearts that are converted to Christ, hearts that are purified as clean vessels so that the new life that was inaugurated in the resurrection and in Pentecost can descend upon them." (Homily, 14 May 1978)

## QUESTIONS FOR REFLECTION

- Thinking about this mystery, what strikes you in light of the message of Scripture and the words of St Oscar Romero?
- Is there a particular intention, or intentions, for which you would like to pray during this decade of the rosary?
- Carry these thoughts and prayers with you as you pray the Our Father, the ten Hail Marys, and the Glory be.

## PRAYER

At the end of this decade, you might wish to pray:

Heavenly Father,
the apostles were transformed
by the gift of the Holy Spirit.
May this same Spirit be poured into the hearts
of every disciple and poured out upon our world.
Help us to deepen our prayer and action,
that the gifts of the Holy Spirit might
bring renewal to the face of the earth
and the lives of those in need.
We ask this through Christ Our Lord. Amen.

Holy Mary, Mother of God – Pray for us
St Oscar Romero – Pray for us

# The Fourth Mystery of Glory -

## The Assumption of Our Blessed Lady, Body and Soul, into Heaven

The Message of the Scriptures - St Paul's First Letter to the Corinthians 15:20-26

Christ has risen from the dead. So also, those who die in Christ shall be raised. It is the Church's ancient faith that the Blessed Virgin Mary, as is fitting for one who carried Christ in her body, was the first to receive the fullness of the resurrection. Mary is the image, example, and hope of every Christian. She has experienced what we shall all come to experience when, having died in Christ, through him we come to share fully the life of his resurrection.

"This journey of Mary in body and soul to heaven is a vibrant sign for all humankind. It tells them that the destiny of the human soul that seeks true happiness is not here on earth. There is a definitive kingdom of heaven beyond our earthly life, but this kingdom is gained only by working in this life and committing ourselves to the fulfilment of God's plan, just as Mary made her earthly life a precise fulfilment of God's plan and an intimate collaboration with the Divine Redeemer in saving the world. ... Mary, then, is the first to be glorified in that heavenly kingdom of which we will all become part in our glorified bodies if after the final judgement we have the happiness of being saved as she was. At the same time, the Council, reflecting on this heavenly perspective where Mary shines forth in all her beauty, looks back to earth and says: this Virgin, now in heaven in body and soul, is not only a figure of our eternal destiny but is also 'a sign of sure hope and solace for the pilgrim people of God.' (*Lumen Gentium* 68) What a beautiful definition of Mary: 'a sign of sure hope and solace.' Thus, as we journey here on earth, as we walk along the dusty and muddy roads of this world, as we undergo the concrete tribulations of life, let us look toward Mary, our sure hope." (Homily, 15 August 1977)

"Like Mary, assumed body and soul into heaven, the Church tells all bodies and all souls about the sublime destiny of humanity. ... The Church presents to the world a Virgin, a womanly body ascending to heaven with all her feminine beauty crowned by the beauty of God. From heaven this Virgin tells all men and women what a high destiny the human body has. ... Mary, assumed body and soul into heaven, is proclaiming, like Saint Paul, that 'the last enemy to be destroyed is death.' (1 Cor 15:26) If death is destroyed by Mary's victorious assumption into heaven, then in all of us the hope remains alive, even though death may seem to extinguish our

life, because our life is sustained by the Spirit of God who has made us immortal and will make us rise up from our graves." (Homily, 15 August 1977)

## QUESTIONS FOR REFLECTION

- Thinking about this mystery, what strikes you in light of the message of Scripture and the words of St Oscar Romero?
- Is there a particular intention, or intentions, for which you would like to pray during this decade of the rosary?
- Carry these thoughts and prayers with you as you pray the Our Father, the ten Hail Marys, and the Glory be.

## PRAYER

At the end of this decade, you might wish to pray:

Heavenly Father,
by the power of your Son's resurrection
Mary, his mother, at the end of her life,
was assumed, body and soul, into heaven.
Her destiny is that of all who die in Christ.
As we live, here on earth, in the hope of heaven
help us to honour the gift of our body,
and to treat every person
with fairness and respect.
We ask this through Christ Our Lord. Amen.

Holy Mary, Mother of God – Pray for us
St Oscar Romero – Pray for us

# The Fifth Mystery of Glory -

## The Coronation of Our Blessed Lady as Queen of Heaven and the Glory of All the Saints

The Message of the Scriptures - The Book of Revelation 12:1-6

The Book of Revelation contains a vision of St John about the end times. The beginning of Chapter 12 describes how he saw a great sign in heaven, a woman clothed with the sun, with the moon at her feet, and a crown of twelve stars on her head. She is pregnant and about to give birth. A dragon appears with its jaws open, wanting to devour the child, the fruit of her womb; but when the moment of birth arrives, the child and the woman are saved. Even so, the persecution by that dragon continues throughout the course of history. This passage of Scripture is understood as an image of Israel, and of the Church, and also, powerfully, of the Blessed Virgin Mary.

"The Church, like Mary, serves humankind by affirming that every person is a child of God, a sister or a brother to be cared for. Mary never tires of offering her protection; she extends her hand as mother and queen and guides us along the path of duty that leads to heaven. The Church is doing the same thing on earth as well. She encourages people to fulfil their obligations, to put aside their sinful ways, and to live their true dignity as children of God. The Church protects her children to the extent that her merits on earth allow, and Mary in heaven also protects them for she is all-powerful through prayer. ... Let us lift up our eyes to Mary, ... let us place our trust in this powerful Virgin who lives and reigns in heaven in body and soul. She makes her power felt through our pilgrim Church with all the beauty of a princess who walks toward her kingdom and hopes for the revelation of her greatness. ... Let us not become discouraged. Rather, let us recognise that the Armour of God in the world bears the immortal spirit of Mary. Let us earnestly cultivate this devotion to Mary." (Homily, 15 August 1977)

"What is the meaning of this vision [of a woman and a dragon in the Book of Revelation]? Scripture scholars have interpreted this as referring to the Church, but many also apply it to the Virgin Mary, mother of the Church. It is all the same because Mary, the Mother of Christ, is the figure of the Church. She is mother of the Church, and whatever touches on the Church touches on Mary. To mention Mary is to mention the Church. This mysterious woman, let us understand, is the Church, the child of Mary. It is the Church founded by Christ to bring Christ to birth in people's hearts, to make Christ be born in those who are converted and who accept him as the Redeemer. It is the Church that suffers the threats of the dragon who wants to kill the fruit of her womb, the dragon who does not want Christ to be born on earth, in people's hearts, in history. ...

In the last days, the Apocalypse tells us, the dragon will be definitively defeated, and the child of Mary will triumph in the kingdom of heaven. ... Blessed are those who are engaged at this time in the battle. Now is the time of struggle here on earth. We lift high the banner of Christ and follow the Lord's teaching." (Homily, 29 September 1977)

## QUESTIONS FOR REFLECTION

- Thinking about this mystery, what strikes you in light of the message of Scripture and the words of St Oscar Romero?
- Is there a particular intention, or intentions, for which you would like to pray during this decade of the rosary?
- Carry these thoughts and prayers with you as you pray the Our Father, the ten Hail Marys, and the Glory be.

## PRAYER

At the end of this decade, you might wish to pray:

Heavenly Father,
by his resurrection, your Son has defeated death and sin.
While the victory against evil has been won,
the devil is still active, promoting division and hatred.
Help us to call on Mary's maternal intercession
as we work to fight the evil of injustice
and oppression in our world.
We ask this through Christ Our Lord. Amen.

Holy Mary, Mother of God – Pray for us
St Oscar Romero – Pray for us

# The Romero
## Mysteries of the Rosary

## Charity, Compassion and Mercy,
## and Justice and Peace

# The Mysteries of Charity

# The First
# Mystery of Charity -

# *The Lord Jesus Teaches Love for Enemies*

The Message of the Scriptures - St Luke 6:27-31

The Lord Jesus speaks to the crowds gathered around him and teaches them a different way of living. This is not the way of hatred or revenge, but the way of love in response to criticism or attack. We are to give to others unreservedly, without seeking any recompense or reward. We are to treat others as we would wish to be treated ourselves.

## From the Words of St Oscar Romero

"Christ came to establish with his resurrection a new human situation of holiness and justice and love. It is not necessary to wait until we die in order to possess heaven. Already on earth love is proclaimed. And as long as there is no love, we will have only that sad reality of people preying like wolves on one another. This is what happens when Christ's love is extinguished in our hearts. Yet it is precisely love that the Church preaches, love even for those who persecute and defame her. As Christ said, 'Love your enemies and pray for those who persecute you.' (Lk 6:27) 'Do good to those who hate you.' (Mt 5:44) This is what we preach: No to vengeance! No to the class struggle! No to violence!" (Homily, 8 May 1977)

"The only force Christ has offered us is the non-violent force of love. Even when we are able to fight, we fight with non-violence, with the force of love. 'Love one another' (Jn 13:34) is something more than conformism; it is something more than tolerating situations with the passivity of the dead. The Church does not want that kind of passivity, and that is why she promotes human dignity and makes people aware of their own dignity. She promotes the equality of all human beings so that people don't allow themselves to be treated as masses, so that we all realise that we are persons, and so that we bestow true dignity on our human personalities. We should not arrogantly impose ourselves with violence and force, but should rather know how to give our personality the human qualities that are truly Christian." (Homily, 12 April 1979)

## QUESTIONS FOR REFLECTION

- Thinking about this mystery, what strikes you in light of the message of Scripture and the words of St Oscar Romero?

- Is there a particular intention, or intentions, for which you would like to pray during this decade of the rosary?

- Carry these thoughts and prayers with you as you pray the Our Father, the ten Hail Marys, and the Glory be.

## PRAYER

At the end of this decade, you might wish to pray:

> Heavenly Father,
> on the cross your Son gave us
> the perfect example of how to love without limit.
> Help us to live this love, especially towards those
> whom we may think of as enemies.
> May we give a sign to the world that even those who may disagree
> can live and love as brothers and sisters.
> We ask this through Christ Our Lord. Amen.
>
> Holy Mary, Mother of God – Pray for us
> St Oscar Romero – Pray for us

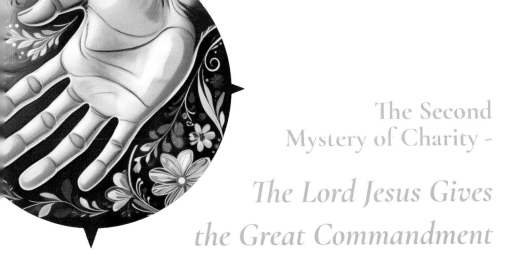

# The Second Mystery of Charity -

# The Lord Jesus Gives the Great Commandment

The Message of the Scriptures - St Matthew 22:34-40

A lawyer, an expert in religious matters, puts a question to the Lord Jesus to try to test him. He asks, 'which is the great commandment in the law?' (Mt 22:36) Knowing that his words will be scrutinised, the Lord replies that the greatest and first commandment is to love God completely, with heart, mind, and soul. Then there is a second commandment, similar to it: to 'love your neighbour as yourself.' (Mt 22:39). This is the foundation, says Jesus, of the Law and the Prophets.

From the Words of St Oscar Romero

"Christ told them…'This is the greatest commandment: You shall love the Lord your God with all your heart, with all your mind, and with all your being. And the second is like it: you shall love your neighbour as yourself.' (Mt 22:37-39) My sisters and brothers, the uniqueness of Christ's statement is not in the words he recited. … But what was unique about Christ was something else, and let us not forget it. Along with this great and grave commandment, 'You shall love God,' he placed at the same level: 'and your neighbour as yourself.' This indeed is unique about Christianity, that you love your neighbour with the same motive with which you love God." (Homily, 29 October 1978)

"Christ said, 'The principal commandment is, 'You shall love the Lord your God with all your heart, with all your mind, with all your strength,' and the second resembles it: 'You shall love your neighbour as yourself.' Loving our neighbour is proof of the love we have for God, and loving God is proof of the love we profess for our neighbour. In a truly Christian heart there cannot be just love for God without love for others, nor can there be just love for others without love for God. … When we pray the Our Father, let no one be excluded from our hearts; let there be no categories dividing people into first and second classes. Rather, let us all rise to the height of God's heart - all of us!" (Homily, 22 April 1979)

## QUESTIONS FOR REFLECTION

- Thinking about this mystery, what strikes you in light of the message of Scripture and the words of St Oscar Romero?
- Is there a particular intention, or intentions, for which you would like to pray during this decade of the rosary?
- Carry these thoughts and prayers with you as you pray the Our Father, the ten Hail Marys, and the Glory be.

## PRAYER

At the end of this decade, you might wish to pray:

Heavenly Father,
your Son teaches us to keep inseparable
our love of you and our love for our neighbour.
Help us to deepen our belief that in loving our
neighbour we are loving you.
Give us open hearts to love you in others,
and to witness to the worth and dignity of each person.
We ask this through Christ Our Lord. Amen.

Holy Mary, Mother of God – Pray for us
St Oscar Romero – Pray for us

# The Third Mystery of Charity –

# The Lord Jesus Calls us to Imitate the Good Samaritan

The Message of the Scriptures - St Luke 10:25-37

The Lord Jesus responds to a question about how to inherit eternal life. He replies by affirming the importance of loving God and loving our neighbour. There follows another question: 'Who is my neighbour?' (Lk 10:29) In response, Jesus tells the parable of a Samaritan who, unlike the priest and the Levite, is the only one to stop and help an injured man. The Samaritan is the one who loves his neighbour. 'You, go and do likewise,' says Jesus. (Lk 10:37)

"It is very easy; indeed, it's almost an evasion to say, 'I go to Church out of love for God, and my neighbour matters little to me.' Remember the parable of the Good Samaritan: the priest and Levite were men of the Church, but they failed in their duty because, in their hurry to get to the temple to pray, they left the poor wounded man on the road; they were not neighbours, declared Christ. (Lk 10:29-37)" (Homily, 29 October 1978)

"We must be concerned for what happens to the poor and the insignificant, but not in just any way. They represent Jesus to the eyes of our faith, which open us up to the poor, the humble, the sick, and the marginalised. When we see Jesus in them, that is transcendence. If we see the poor only as foolish rivals who are going to spoil my party, then naturally they bother us. But when we embrace them, as Christ embraced the leper, (Mk 1:40-41) and when we lift them up as the Good Samaritan lifted up the wounded man on the highway, (Lk 10:33-35) this is transcendence because what is done for them is done for Christ. (Mt 25:40) Only transcendence can give us the perspective for social justice: Christ among the little ones." (Homily, 30 September 1979)

## QUESTIONS FOR REFLECTION

- Thinking about this mystery, what strikes you in light of the message of Scripture and the words of St Oscar Romero?
- Is there a particular intention, or intentions, for which you would like to pray during this decade of the rosary?
- Carry these thoughts and prayers with you as you pray the Our Father, the ten Hail Marys, and the Glory be.

## PRAYER

At the end of this decade, you might wish to pray:

Heavenly Father,
we are told by your Son,
not to walk by on the other side of the road, seemingly indifferent,
when we encounter suffering and need in our sisters and brothers.
Expand our hearts with a greater love for you,
and help us to express this love in a greater love for our neighbour.
We ask this through Christ Our Lord. Amen.

Holy Mary, Mother of God – Pray for us
St Oscar Romero – Pray for us

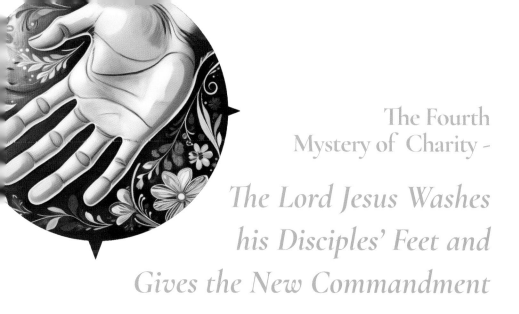

# The Fourth Mystery of Charity -

# The Lord Jesus Washes his Disciples' Feet and Gives the New Commandment

The Message of the Scriptures - St John 13:1-16, 31-35

During the Last Supper with his disciples, the night before he died for us, the Lord puts a towel around his waist and washes his disciples' feet. It was unthinkable that Jesus should do this, adopting the role of a slave, and Simon Peter protests. However, Jesus does this as an example of service that they should follow. Only in this way could they have a share in his mission. Jesus gives them a new commandment: 'love one another: just as I have loved you, you also are to love one another. By this all people will know that you are my disciples; if you have love one for another.' (Jn 13:34-35)

"'Before the feast of Passover, Jesus knew that his hour had come to pass'- that is 'pass over' – 'from this world to the Father. He loved his own in the world, and he loved them to the end.' (Jn 13:1) In all of history no one has ever encountered a love that was so - how to say it? - so crazy, so exaggerated: giving to the point of being crucified on a cross. There is no friend who has given his life for another friend with such an outpouring of suffering and love as Christ our Lord. This is the setting of our Passover. That is why Christ tells us that the sign of the Christian is living the new commandment he gives us. It is a commandment that ... becomes fresh in our memory and our lives: 'As I have loved you, so you also should love one another.' (Jn 13:34)" (Homily, 23 March 1978)

"When Christ stood up again after washing his disciples' feet, he said to them, 'I have given you an example. You call me "teacher and master," and rightly so, for I am indeed your teacher and your master. Therefore, do what I have shown you: wash one another's feet.' (Jn 13:13-15) He meant this not in a literal sense but in the sense of serving others because in Jesus' time washing feet was the work of a slave. When a guest or a visitor arrived, the slave had to wash his feet - it was a duty of slaves. Jesus teaches us that nothing is humiliating when there is love. Peter was scandalised and said to Jesus, 'How are you, Lord, going to wash my feet since you're so great and I'm so insignificant?' 'Let it be,' Jesus told him, 'because unless I wash you, you will have no part with me.' (Jn 13:6,8) Only then did Peter understand that this gesture of humility was the key to entering into communion with Jesus. Sisters and brothers, it is only with this key of humility and service that we can enter into the civilisation of love. Those who are proud, greedy, and haughty only hate. Those who are humble and generous know how to love. Put aside pride, avarice and arrogance. Love humility and self-denial. When you have love and humility in your heart, you can be happy and you can be holy." (Homily, 12 April 1979)

## QUESTIONS FOR REFLECTION

- Thinking about this mystery, what strikes you in light of the message of Scripture and the words of St Oscar Romero?

- Is there a particular intention, or intentions, for which you would like to pray during this decade of the rosary?

- Carry these thoughts and prayers with you as you pray the Our Father, the ten Hail Marys, and the Glory be.

## PRAYER

At the end of this decade, you might wish to pray:

Heavenly Father,
your Son left us an example
when he washed his disciples' feet.
May we follow his example of loving service,
and, as we try to live the new commandment,
help us to return the love he gives us
with a generous love of others.
Teach us to be servants and make us humble and gentle.
We ask this through Christ Our Lord. Amen.

Holy Mary, Mother of God – Pray for us
St Oscar Romero – Pray for us

# The Lord Jesus
# Recommissions the Apostle Peter

The Message of the Scriptures - St John 21:1-19

After rising from the dead, the Lord Jesus appears to his disciples by the Sea of Galilee. The disciples are fishing and Jesus instructs them to cast their nets on the right side of their boat. They catch an enormous quantity of fish. Realising 'it is the Lord,' (Jn 21:7) Peter jumps into the water, trying to reach Jesus first, ashamed that he denied Jesus before his crucifixion. The Lord makes a charcoal fire on the beach and cooks some fish for the disciples' breakfast. Afterwards, Jesus asks Peter three times 'Do you love me?' Peter replies, three times, 'Yes Lord; you know that I love you.' Then Jesus indicates that Peter will follow a path that would lead him to martyrdom.

"And then there is the sentence, 'If we deny him, he will also deny us.' But there is something else: 'if we are unfaithful, he remains faithful.' (2 Tim 2:13a) What a great consolation! Even when we betray him, if we seek him once again, we will find him with open arms. All is forgotten, as with Peter on the morning of the resurrection. Even though Christ witnessed Peter's cowardly negotiations on Holy Thursday night, he simply asks him, 'Do you love me?' (Jn 21:15) Peter, ashamed and repentant, responds, 'Yes, Lord, I love you. What occurred the other night was pure weakness. I deserve to be punished.' And Christ does not reproach him for his sin. He remains faithful. Every sinner and every traitor who has drawn away from Christ should remember this: 'If we have been unfaithful, he remains faithful.' This is consoling, sisters and brothers, for me as a sinner and for each of you as sinners! Despite all our weaknesses and defects, we have found him; he has forgiven us; he loves us; all is forgotten 'for he cannot deny himself.' (2 Tim 2:13b) This is a truly profound reason, for otherwise he would cease to be God, he would cease to be Redeemer." (Homily, 9 October 1977)

"Everything begins with God's love. If Christ came as the Saviour of humankind, it was by the initiative of the Father. 'God so loved the world that he sent his own Son.' He told him, 'Go, Son, become a man. Join them in their history. Enter into their sufferings. Carry on your shoulders the sins of all. Climb up with them to Calvary, and in your crucifixion I will behold the reparation of all their sins.'" (Homily, 25 March 1979)

## QUESTIONS FOR REFLECTION

- Thinking about this mystery, what strikes you in light of the message of Scripture and the words of St Oscar Romero?

- Is there a particular intention, or intentions, for which you would like to pray during this decade of the rosary?

- Carry these thoughts and prayers with you as you pray the Our Father, the ten Hail Marys, and the Glory be.

## PRAYER

At the end of this decade, you might wish to pray:

Heavenly Father,
like the apostle Peter
we too, sometimes, can struggle to be faithful
to you and to the call of your Son, Jesus.
Renew within us the gift of the Holy Spirit.
Help us always to be able to return in repentance
and receive again your healing and mercy.
Make us open-hearted in our acceptance of others.
We ask this through Christ Our Lord. Amen.

Holy Mary, Mother of God – Pray for us
St Oscar Romero – Pray for us

# The Mysteries of Compassion and Mercy

# The First Mystery of Compassion and Mercy -

## *The Lord Jesus Calls Matthew the Tax Collector*

The Message of the Scriptures - St Matthew 9:9-13

The Lord Jesus sees Matthew, a tax collector, and says to him 'Follow me,' and Mathew rises and follows him. (Mt 9:9) While at table with Jesus that evening, there are also other tax collectors and sinners present. A Pharisee asks one of the disciples why his teacher eats with such people. Jesus replies, 'Those who are well have no need of a physician, but those who are sick. Go and learn what this means: 'I desire mercy, and not sacrifice. For I came not to call the righteous, but sinners.' (Mt 9:12-13)

"The tax collectors were repugnant types, compared in the Gospels with publicans and sinners, harlots and thieves, all sorts of miscreants. To one of these Christ calls, 'Come, follow me.' (Mt 9:9) And Matthew leaves his customs post; profit and extortion no longer matter to him. He follows Jesus and in gratitude prepares a meal for him, a little supper, naturally with his friends; the folks around him were lowlife - thieves, publicans, other tax collectors. Who else could the poor man invite? Christ doesn't refuse even though he was aware of the puritanical attitude of the Pharisees, who condemned any socialising with Jews who failed to keep the law and so were called sinners. The Pharisees did not mix with these people; they wouldn't even shake the hand of a tax collector or a publican. Even though in their hearts they did worse things, they took care to preserve appearances. Christ is not afraid of their criticism or people's attitudes. When he goes and eats with the outcasts, this is seen by the Pharisees as something awful. They say to Jesus' disciples, 'Why does your teacher eat with tax collectors and sinners?' Jesus overhears their question and defends his stance: 'Those who are well do not need a physician, but the sick do. I have not come to seek the righteous - they're already safe. I have come to seek sinners. I am the Saviour of the world.'" (Homily, 11 June 1978)

"What is mercy? Mercy is the most perfect expression of love. It is love as surrender, as forgiveness, as justice, as living in peace with others. Mercy is not the pride of the Pharisees who despise the outcasts; rather, it is the embrace of God who, though super-rich, has come to seek out both the poor and those who don't want to sit down and eat with them. Mercy is goodness expressed in deeds and not in words. All of us understand mercy better because we've all done some small act of mercy for others, and above all because we've all been the recipients of mercy. If God had not been merciful to us when we fell into so many sins, where would we be?

If God did not have the mercy to forgive us before he died, where would we go? And perhaps also in our human relationships we've known many acts of mercy done by us or done for us. Blessed are those whose lives have been filled with many merciful acts! That is what God desires!" (Homily, 11 June 1978)

## QUESTIONS FOR REFLECTION

- Thinking about this mystery, what strikes you in light of the message of Scripture and the words of St Oscar Romero?
- Is there a particular intention, or intentions, for which you would like to pray during this decade of the rosary?
- Carry these thoughts and prayers with you as you pray the Our Father, the ten Hail Marys, and the Glory be.

## PRAYER

At the end of this decade, you might wish to pray:

Heavenly Father, thank you that, through your Son,
you call us to yourself, even while we are sinners.
As we seek your mercy,
help us also to be missionaries of mercy to others
by our compassion and forgiveness.
Widen our hearts so that we do not place limits
on how and where the Holy Spirit is at work.
We ask this through Christ Our Lord. Amen.

Holy Mary, Mother of God – Pray for us
St Oscar Romero – Pray for us

# The Second Mystery of Compassion and Mercy-

## *The Woman Anoints the Feet of the Lord Jesus*

The Message of the Scriptures - St Luke 7:36-50

The Lord Jesus enters the house of a Pharisee, and a woman, known to be a sinner, comes and kneels behind him. She is crying and her tears fall on his feet. She wipes the tears away with her hair, kisses his feet, and anoints them with ointment. Simon, the Pharisee who invited Jesus, complains: 'If this man were a prophet, he would have known who and what sort of woman this is who is touching him, for she is a sinner.' (Lk 7:39) Jesus explains that those forgiven the biggest debts love the most. The woman showed Jesus great love and kindness, more than the host did. From this great love, we know she had been pardoned for her many sins. Jesus says to the woman 'your sins are forgiven ... your faith has saved you; go in peace.' (Lk 7:50)

"What time is more solemn than that moment of silence in the confessional? The soul, weighed down by sins it can no longer bear, hears the priest proclaim the words that Christ spoke to Magdalene: 'Rise up! You are forgiven! I forgive you.' (Lk 7:47) ... We all go to confession because we need that service of consolation that no earthly wisdom can give. There are no words so consoling and healing as those pronounced by the priest: 'I forgive you in the name of Christ, the forgiver.'" (Homily, 10 December 1977)

"In Jesus' time the respectable folk kept pointing at the prostitute Mary Magdalene even when she was weeping for her sins: 'Look, if he were really a prophet, he would realise who that woman is who is touching him.' (Lk 7:39) But Christ came to her defence: 'She is no longer a sinner for she has loved much and she has repented of her faults; she is already Saint Mary Magdalene.' (Lk 7:47) The sins of the past no longer count; they dissolve. That's why Christian justification is called rebirth. ... All those who repent of their faults leave behind the evil of their past lives as if shedding an old skin and donning a new one; they now have nothing to do with what was left in the past! Think of how the butterfly is born again as it leaves its cocoon and becomes a new creature. Blessed be God! This is the generosity of God. We cannot understand it because all we know is how to utter the cruel words, 'I forgive, but I don't forget.' That is not Christian. God forgives and forgets." (Homily, 24 September 1978)

## QUESTIONS FOR REFLECTION

- Thinking about this mystery, what strikes you in light of the message of Scripture and the words of St Oscar Romero?
- Is there a particular intention, or intentions, for which you would like to pray during this decade of the rosary?
- Carry these thoughts and prayers with you as you pray the Our Father, the ten Hail Marys, and the Glory be.

## PRAYER

At the end of this decade, you might wish to pray:

Heavenly Father,
you love us so much
that you sent your Son to bring us new life
by his cross and resurrection.
Help us, who are in need of forgiveness,
and have been forgiven so much,
to refrain from grudges, blame, and revenge,
and instead to love generously and compassionately in return.
We ask this through Christ Our Lord. Amen.

Holy Mary, Mother of God – Pray for us
St Oscar Romero – Pray for us

# The Third Mystery of Compassion and Mercy -

## *The Lord Jesus Encounters the Rich Young Man*

The Message of the Scriptures - St Mark 10:17-22

A man, unnamed in the Gospel, but referred to as the 'rich young man,' comes and kneels before the Lord Jesus. He asks Jesus, whom he calls the 'good teacher,' (Mk 10:17) what he must do to inherit eternal life. The Lord Jesus reminds him that God alone is good, and that he must keep the commandments. The rich young man replies 'Teacher, all these I have kept from my youth.' (Mk 10:20) Jesus 'looking at him, loved him,' (Mk 10:21) and says he must sell his possessions and give the money to the poor. Then, Jesus says, 'follow me.' (Mk 10:21) The man goes away sorrowful because he was a person of many possessions.

"This moving gospel narrative continues with the young man's response [about keeping the commandments]: 'All this I have done since I was a child!' And it becomes even more moving when it describes Jesus as 'looking on him with great affection.' (Mk 10:20-21a) A dialogue of kindness! How I wish that, if the Lord were to see me today, he would look on me with affection and not with the reproachful look that he must have directed at the hypocrites, the Pharisees, the adulterers, the sinners. When Christ took on a severe look with his enemies, it must have been as terrible as a scourging, but the look of love that Christ had for this young person who fulfilled the law of God was a caress. There is no caress like that of the face of Christ smiling at me, satisfied that I am doing what I ought to do." (Homily, 14 October 1979)

"Christ had more to say to the young man: 'You're lacking one thing.' (Mk 10:21b) Now Christ was challenging the natural goodness that people have. It is not enough to be good; it is not enough to refrain from doing evil. Christianity is something very positive and not simply negation. There are many people who say, 'I don't kill. I don't steal. I don't hurt anybody.' That's not enough. You're still lacking much! The young man's goodness was still deficient, and it became clear when Christ told him what he was lacking: 'Go, sell what you have, and give the money to the poor, and you will have treasure in heaven. Then, come, follow me.' Sadly, the gospel says that the young man's 'face fell and he went away sad because he was very rich.' (Mk 10:21c-22) It is not that Christ had a grudge against the rich, nor is it true that the Church or the Church's preaching rails against them. That is not the case. We have just said that Christ 'looked on the young man with love,' (Mk 10:21a) and because he loved him, he taught him the true way." (Homily, 14 October 1979)

## QUESTIONS FOR REFLECTION

- Thinking about this mystery, what strikes you in light of the message of Scripture and the words of St Oscar Romero?
- Is there a particular intention, or intentions, for which you would like to pray during this decade of the rosary?
- Carry these thoughts and prayers with you as you pray the Our Father, the ten Hail Marys, and the Glory be.

## PRAYER

At the end of this decade, you might wish to pray:

Heavenly Father,
we desire to follow your Son,
and to be captured by his gaze of steady love.
Help us to overcome the obstacles
which prevent us from giving ourselves
more fully and freely to the Lord Jesus.
Teach us to love every person,
no matter what their situation in life happens to be.
We ask this through Christ Our Lord. Amen.

Holy Mary, Mother of God – Pray for us
St Oscar Romero – Pray for us

# The Fourth Mystery of Compassion and Mercy -

## The Lord Jesus Meets the Woman Caught in Adultery

The Message of the Scriptures - John 8:1-11

A woman caught in the act of adultery is brought before the Lord Jesus. Those in authority want to punish her, according to the law, by stoning her. To test Jesus, they ask his opinion. He replies that the one without sin should be 'the first to throw a stone at her.' (Jn 8:7) One by one, the accusers depart until the woman is alone with Jesus. He asks her whether anyone has condemned her and she replies that no one has. Jesus says to her, 'Neither do I condemn you; go, and from now on, sin no more.' (Jn 8:11)

From the Words of St Oscar Romero

"I can find no more beautiful example of saving human dignity than the figure of the sinless Jesus face to face with the adulterous woman who was surprised in the act and humiliated. Those who caught her want to sentence her to stoning. Without saying a word Jesus reproaches those who would judge her with their own sins, and then he asks the woman, 'Has no one condemned you?' 'No one, sir.' 'Then neither do I condemn you. But sin no more.' (Jn 8:10-11) Strength, but tenderness. Human dignity comes first." (Homily, 23 March 1980)

"When this woman was caught, the Pharisees and scribes were debating how she should die, whether by stoning or strangulation or some other way. Thus they said to Jesus, 'This woman was caught in adultery. Our law says she should die. What do you say?' (Jn 8:4-5) In other words, they were asking him, 'How should we kill her?' Jesus was not concerned about the legalistic details. Calmly rising above the malice of those trying to entrap him, he began to write on the ground, like someone scribbling notes on a piece of paper. The crowd kept insisting until Jesus responded with cleverness and wisdom, 'Let the one among you who has no sin be the first to cast a stone.' (Jn 8:7) He touched their conscience. They were witnesses of the deed, and according to the ancient laws the witnesses were to throw the first stones. As they examined their own consciences, however, they realised that they were witnesses of their own sins. Thus was the woman's dignity saved. God does not save sin, but he does save the dignity of a woman submerged in sin. He has come in love precisely to save sinners, and here we have a perfect case. Converting the woman is much better than stoning her. Forgiving her and saving her is much better than condemning her. ... Look closely at this gospel so as to learn something of how considerate Jesus is with the other person. He always sees the person, no matter how sinful, as a child of God, an image of the Lord. He does not condemn, but only forgives. He does not condone the sin - he strongly rejects it - but he knows how to condemn the sin and save the sinner. ... By giving true primacy to human dignity, Jesus is a source of peace. People feel they matter to Jesus, who has no sin and no need to repent. Returning to him with sincerity is the greatest joy a human being can have." (Homily, 23 March 1980)

## QUESTIONS FOR REFLECTION

- Thinking about this mystery, what strikes you in light of the message of Scripture and the words of St Oscar Romero?
- Is there a particular intention, or intentions, for which would like to pray during this decade of the rosary?
- Carry these thoughts and prayers with you as you pray Our Father, the ten Hail Marys, and the Glory be.

## PRAYER

At the end of this decade, you might wish to pray:

> Heavenly Father,
> your Son reveals divine mercy
> and compassion to every person.
> Help us to be compassionate, as you,
> Father, are compassionate.
> May we seek forgiveness for our own sins and not judge others.
> Open us to receive the power of your healing,
> and to be instruments of healing for others.
> We ask this through Christ Our Lord. Amen.
>
> Holy Mary, Mother of God – Pray for us
> St Oscar Romero – Pray for us

# The Fifth Mystery of Compassion and Mercy -

## *The Lord Jesus Teaches About the Prodigal Son and the Forgiving Father*

The Message of the Scriptures – St Luke 15:11-32

The Lord Jesus teaches about God's patient love through the parable of the father with two sons. The younger son asks for his inheritance and leaves home to squander his money in a life of indulgence. When he hits rock bottom, he returns home. His father is waiting, looking out for him, and welcomes him with a feast. The older son, however, cannot accept the celebration of his brother's return, while he, who has always been dutiful, is overlooked. However, the father says, 'Son you are always with me, and all that is mine is yours. It was fitting to celebrate and be glad, for this your brother was dead, and is alive; he was lost, and is found.' (Lk 15:31-32)

"Blessed is that moment. The gospel describes it for us with incomparable words: 'While he was still a long way off, his father caught sight of him, and was filled with compassion. He ran to his son, embraced him and kissed him.' (Lk 15:20) This is the vengeance of God. When his son tries to beg pardon – 'Father, I have sinned' (Lk 15:21) - he does not let him speak. He calls his servants to come and clothe his son in the finest garments, for the lad, who was dead, has come to life again. There is great joy, as Christ says ... 'There will be more joy in heaven over one sinner who repents than over ninety-nine righteous people who have no need of repentance.' (Lk 15:7) The Church is there for sinners. As Saint Paul said, 'Christ has come for sinners, and for me first of all.' (1 Tim 1:15) ... [This] is the return home where love awaits us with open arms. He will not reject me, no matter how great my sins. I repeat this, sisters and brothers, because during these days some sinners have confided in me and asked, 'Will the Lord forgive me if my sins are so great?' And I have told them what I here tell you in public: 'Of course he will forgive you. If your sins are great, greater still is God's goodness,' as the missionaries sing. No sin can extinguish the fire of God's love. To the contrary, this love of God is like a fire that will burn away all the underbrush of sin that exists in the world." (Homily, 11 September 1977)

"I would like us just to sit in silence and remember that the story of that son is our own personal story. Each one of you, and myself as well, can see in the parable of the prodigal son something of our own history. ... The God of love invites us to live in his house, but we capriciously and crazily run away, trying to enjoy a life without God, which is sin. Even so, God patiently waits until the day when his son returns home. When the son, overcome with misery and abandoned by others, remembers that there is no greater love than God's, he returns. Though the son expects to find

God resentful and rejecting, he finds him instead welcoming him with outstretched arms, ready to throw a party to celebrate his return." (Homily, 16 March 1980)

## QUESTIONS FOR REFLECTION

- Thinking about this mystery, what strikes you in light of the message of Scripture and the words of St Oscar Romero?
- Is there a particular intention, or intentions, for which you would like to pray during this decade of the rosary?
- Carry these thoughts and prayers with you as you pray the Our Father, the ten Hail Marys, and the Glory be.

## PRAYER

At the end of this decade, you might wish to pray:

Heavenly Father, you have given us the freedom
to accept or reject your love for us.
Help us always to say 'yes' to your love,
shown to us in your beloved Son Jesus.
When we stray from you,
bring us back with your compassionate, patient loving.
Give us generous hearts towards those distant from you
and your Church, and in need of mercy.
We ask this through Christ Our Lord. Amen.

Holy Mary, Mother of God – Pray for us
St Oscar Romero – Pray for us

# The Mysteries of Justice and Peace

The Message of the Scriptures - St Luke 4:16-22

The Lord Jesus enters the Synagogue at Nazareth and reads from the scroll of the Prophet Isaiah, 'The Spirit of the Lord is upon me, because he has anointed me to proclaim good news to the poor ... liberty to captives ... recovering of sight to the blind ... liberty [to] those who are oppressed ... [and] the year of the Lord's favour.' (Lk 4:18-19) When he finishes reading, Jesus rolls up the scroll and sits down. Everyone in the synagogue fixes their eyes on him. 'Today,' he said, 'this Scripture has been fulfilled in your hearing.' (Lk 4:21)

"The anointing of Christ was therefore an inner anointing, an anointing that did not come from outside but rather from the originating principle, so that it was a marvellous work of the Holy Spirit. ... 'The Spirit is upon me.' (Is 61:1) Commenting on this prophecy of Isaiah, the Messiah declared, 'Today this Scripture passage is fulfilled. The Spirit of God is upon me. (Lk 4:21) I am the marvellous work of the Holy Spirit. While I appear among you as just another man, I have the Spirit's anointing, and I bear within me the person of God who gives divine value to all my human acts. If my human arms, when nailed to a cross, are going to have power to save the world from all its sins, it is not by the blood of a son of Mary; it is because this son of Mary has been anointed as the true Son of God and everything he suffers has divine value.'" (Homily, 12 April 1979)

"I repeat, sisters and brothers, what I told you once before, precisely when we were afraid that one day we would be without the radio: the best microphone of God is Christ, and the best microphone of Christ is the Church, and the Church is all of you! Each one of you, from your own position and your own vocation, should live the faith intensely whether you are married, a religious, a bishop, a priest, a student, an undergrad, a labourer, a worker, a market vendor. In your own particular situation you should feel that you are a true microphone of God our Lord. ... The passage read by Christ, tells of all the marvels of liberation: 'The Spirit is upon me because God has anointed me.' (Lk 4:18a) 'He has anointed me!' Christ is the anointed One - that's what 'Christ' or 'Messiah' means. ... He is the anointed One, the one who has been assumed by and steeped in the Holy Spirit. As the anointed One, he is the fullness of the Spirit of God. ... 'He has anointed me and has sent me to bring glad tidings to the poor.' (Lk 4:18b) This is the mission of Christ: to bring good news to the poor, to those who receive only bad news, to those who receive only abuse from the powerful, to those who can only watch the riches that delight others pass them by. It is for these that the Lord comes, to make them happy and to tell them, 'Do not be greedy. Consider yourselves happy and wealthy because of the great gift brought to you by the One who "being rich became poor" in order to be with you. (2 Cor 8:9) Realise that the greatest happiness is taking part in the joy that God shares with his poor.'" (Homily, 27 January 1980)

## QUESTIONS FOR REFLECTION

- Thinking about this mystery, what strikes you in light of the message of Scripture and the words of St Oscar Romero?
- Is there a particular intention, or intentions, for which you would like to pray during this decade of the rosary?
- Carry these thoughts and prayers with you as you pray the Our Father, the ten Hail Marys, and the Glory be.

## PRAYER

At the end of this decade, you might wish to pray:

Heavenly Father, by the grace of baptism and confirmation
we are anointed with the Holy Spirit to live like your Son.
Help us to consider today
how we can proclaim good news, freedom, new sight, and fresh hope.
May we share the Gospel of the Lord's favour with our
brothers and sisters through our words and deeds.
We ask this through Christ Our Lord. Amen.

Holy Mary, Mother of God – Pray for us
St Oscar Romero – Pray for us

# The Lord Jesus
# Imparts the Beatitudes

The Message of the Scriptures - St Matthew 5:1-12

The Lord Jesus goes up the mountain with his disciples, sits down and imparts to the people the Beatitudes, the realities of blessedness in the kingdom of God. Blessed are the poor in spirit, those who mourn, and who are meek, for theirs is the kingdom of heaven, they shall be comforted and inherit the earth. Blessed are those hungering and thirsting for justice, for that righreousness which is morally at one with God and with others, for they shall be satisfied. Blessed are those who are merciful and pure in heart, for they shall receive mercy and see God. Blessed are the peacemakers, those persecuted for the sake of justice and righteousness, and those persecuted for the sake of Christ, for they are children of God, theirs is the kingdom of heaven, where their reward will be great.

"Blessed are those, then, who take advantage of their poverty to open themselves to hope. This passage opens us to hope in the midst of tribulations, but not to preach conformity; the Church is never conformist! Rather, she tells people ... that the struggle here on this earth should not have as its goal the greedy desire to possess. That simply depersonalises people and leaves them morally underdeveloped. Instead, people should work and struggle for the welfare of themselves and their families. Their hearts must be open to hope, and their love must be open to the service of others. 'Blessed are the meek,' Jesus says, 'for they will inherit the land.' (Mt 5:4) ... This land of justice and love that Christians hope for is not found here in this world, but this world ought to reflect this justice and love. The full reality lies beyond history and will be our destiny.

"'Blessed are those who mourn.' (Mt 5:5) They mourn because they do not have the earthly joys that others have. They mourn because they see people's sins and ask for God's forgiveness. Blessed are those who mourn with these noble feelings because they will receive the greatest of comforts: they will see that God forgives his people, and they will understand that there are joys that do not belong to this earth. 'Blessed are those who hunger and thirst for justice.' (Mt 5:6) Justice in the biblical sense means a good relationship between God and humankind. It also means God's victory over human evil. The truly just want to maintain their relationship with God so that it is not corrupted by earthly sin. The truly just are grieved that so many people lack a good relationship with God because they have divinised something that is not really the true God.

"'Blessed are the merciful, for they will receive mercy.' (Mt 5:7) This is one of the most profound biblical desires. Humans are not made for vengeance, for hatred, for violence, but for reconciliation, for love, for forgiveness. We will be forgiven in the measure that we forgive. ... Blessed are the merciful and generous hearts that are instruments of peace and that sow harmony where there is discord. (Mt 5:8)

"'Blessed are the clean of heart.' The gospel here refers to the sincerity that caused conflict between Jesus and the Pharisees. The Pharisees were concerned only about an exterior, ritualistic, legalistic purity. ... Jesus called them hypocrites. 'What good is it to clean the outside of the plate if inside it is dirty?' Clean of heart refers to those who sincerely cleanse their hearts, because 'one is not made unclean by the things that enter the stomach or by eating with unclean hands, but rather one is made unclean by the things that come forth from the heart: evil thoughts and desires and avarice. These are the things that make a person unclean.' (Mt 15:17-20) This, then, is a call to sincerity.

"'Blessed are the peacemakers, for they shall be called children of God.' (Mt 5:9) My sisters and brothers, this is a time when God wants his many children to work on behalf of peace and not violence. He wants us to make peace not just a facade but a true work of justice and love. And finally, 'Blessed are those who are persecuted for the sake of justice, for theirs is the kingdom of heaven.' (Mt 5:10) ... Persecution has been the inheritance of the Church down through the centuries, but now it is the time to say that those who suffer this persecution are blessed." (Homily, 29 January 1978)

## QUESTIONS FOR REFLECTION

- Thinking about this mystery, what strikes you in light of the message of Scripture and the words of St Oscar Romero?
- Is there a particular intention, or intentions, for which you would like to pray during this decade of the rosary?
- Carry these thoughts and prayers with you as you pray the Our Father, the ten Hail Marys, and the Glory be.

## PRAYER

At the end of this decade, you might wish to pray:

Heavenly Father,
by the gift of the Holy Spirit
open our hearts to the Beatitudes taught by your Son.
Help us to change and to shape our lives
according to the true values of your kingdom.
Strengthen us to be witnesses on earth to the truth of the Gospel.
We ask this through Christ Our Lord. Amen.

Holy Mary, Mother of God – Pray for us
St Oscar Romero – Pray for us

# The Third Mystery of Justice and Peace -

## The Lord Jesus Calls Zacchaeus to Conversion

The Message of the Scriptures – St Luke 19:1-10

The Lord Jesus enters Jericho and meets Zacchaeus, a tax collector, who has climbed a tree to get a better view of Jesus. When Jesus sees Zacchaeus, he calls him down from the tree and tells him he will stay at his house. Although judged badly by others, his meeting with Jesus changes Zacchaeus. 'Behold, Lord,' he says, 'half of my goods I give to the poor. And if I have defrauded anyone of anything, I restore it four-fold.' (Lk 19:8) 'Today,' said Jesus, 'salvation has come to this house.' (Lk 19:9)

"Our Lord is walking through the streets of Jericho. In the city there is a rich man, the chief tax collector, who has an earnest desire to see Jesus. Since he is short in stature, he climbs a tree, never imagining that our Lord, cheered by the crowds, would notice him. But as he passes under the tree, he lifts his eyes, sees him, and calls him by name: 'Zacchaeus, come down for I want to go to your house. I want to stay at your house.' (Lk 19:5) When Zacchaeus hears that voice, he comes down. But it is not mere curiosity that motivates him. On hearing the malicious comments of those who see Jesus enter his house, Zacchaeus shows himself to be a man who for some time has felt the weight of sin on his conscience. Before Jesus he declares: 'I am going to give half my property to the poor, and if I have cheated anybody I will pay him back four times the amount.' Our Lord congratulates him for that: 'Zacchaeus, today happiness has come to your house.' (Lk 19:8-9) This aspect of the gospel is very interesting because it helps us to see that true conversion expresses itself in deeds." (Homily, 30 October 1977)

"It is not enough just to say that one repents of a sin; it is also necessary to repair the harm that was done. Since that collector of taxes and chief publican had often extorted money in carrying out his job, he felt the need to give half of his goods to the poor and to reimburse fourfold those he had defrauded. Sisters and brothers, the Gospel calls us to such a conversion, a conversion that doesn't just remain in sentiments, but that leads to total change and teaches us the need to share. The ... world's goods are created by God for the benefit of all and therefore must correspond to this plan of God. ... Let us welcome this word and take care that it is not something that is kept in a broken sack; let it not be scattered along the wayside or fall among thorns or onto stones. Rather,

let it fall on good ground so that it can take root and give thirty, sixty, and a hundredfold. (Mk 4:1-8)" (Homily, 30 October 1977)

## QUESTIONS FOR REFLECTION

- Thinking about this mystery, what strikes you in light of the message of Scripture and the words of St Oscar Romero?
- Is there a particular intention, or intentions, for which you would like to pray during this decade of the rosary?
- Carry these thoughts and prayers with you as you pray the Our Father, the ten Hail Marys, and the Glory be.

## PRAYER

At the end of this decade, you might wish to pray:

Heavenly Father,
like Zacchaeus we want to see Jesus your Son.
Help us to search for him, and to listen for his voice as
he calls us by name and comes to dwell
in the house of our heart.
By our encounter with Jesus,
help us to recognise our need for conversion
and to put right the injustices in our lives.
We ask this through Christ Our Lord. Amen.

Holy Mary, Mother of God – Pray for us
St Oscar Romero – Pray for us

# The Fourth Mystery of Justice and Peace -
# The Lord Jesus Teaches about the Final Judgement

The Message of the Scriptures - St Matthew 25:31-46

The Lord Jesus teaches about the final judgement, when we will be called to give an account of our lives. The extent to which we have loved and served Christ will be shown by the extent to which we have given food to the hungry, water to the thirsty, welcome to the stranger, clothing to the naked, concern for the sick and the prisoner. Jesus concludes, 'Truly, I say to you, as you did it to one of the least of these of my brothers and sisters you did it to me.' (Mt 25:40)

From the Words of St Oscar Romero

"'Whatever you did to one of these poor sisters or brothers of mine, you did it to me.' (Mt 25:40) How close Christ has been to us, and how often we've failed to recognise him! We should discover the face of Christ in every sister and brother we greet, in every friend whose hand we shake, in every beggar who asks for bread, in every worker who seeks to exercise his right to organise a union, in every campesino [a farm worker] who looks for work in the coffee groves. If we recognise Christ in them, then we won't rob them, deceive them, or deny their rights. They are Christ, and whatever is done to them Christ will take as done to him. Christ is living among us." (Homily, 3 December 1978)

"'Whatever you do for one of them, you do for me.' (Mt 25:40) The transcendence that the Church preaches is not alienation; it is not about going to heaven and thinking about eternal life while forgetting the problems of earth. Rather, it is the transcendence of the human heart; it is getting involved with children, it is getting involved with the poor, it is getting involved with the homeless and with the sick folk in their huts and their shacks. It is sharing in the depths of their miserable situation so that they can transcend it, raise themselves up, and flourish. It is telling them, 'You are not rubbish. You are not outcasts.' Quite to the contrary, it is telling them, 'You are invaluable. You are worth as much as those who live in the great mansions that you see but can never own. You are equal. You are a human person like everyone else, an image of God. You also are called to heaven.' This is the transcendence that is a true dimension of those who are great." (Homily, 23 September 1979)

## QUESTIONS FOR REFLECTION

- Thinking about this mystery, what strikes you in light of the message of Scripture and the words of St Oscar Romero?
- Is there a particular intention, or intentions, for which you would like to pray during this decade of the rosary?
- Carry these thoughts and prayers with you as you pray the Our Father, the ten Hail Marys, and the Glory be.

## PRAYER

At the end of this decade, you might wish to pray:

Heavenly Father, your Son asks us
to see him present in every person.
Help us not to be indifferent
when faced with the need of others,
but to feed Jesus in the hungry,
to give him drink in the thirsty,
to clothe him in the naked
and to visit him in the sick and in those imprisoned.
May we keep always in mind that
what we do to others, we do to Jesus.
We ask this through Christ Our Lord. Amen.

Holy Mary, Mother of God – Pray for us
St Oscar Romero – Pray for us

## The Fifth Mystery of Justice and Peace -

## The Risen Lord Brings the Gift of Peace

The Message of the Scriptures - St John 20:19-21

The risen Lord Jesus appears to his disciples and says to them 'Peace be with you.' (Jn 20:19) He shows them his hands and side and the disciples rejoice to see Jesus in his resurrected body. He says again to them, 'Peace be with you. As the Father has sent me, even so I am sending you.' (Jn 20:21)

"'No to violence! Yes to peace!'... Peace was the greeting of the risen Lord, freed from the chains of sin which had now been redeemed, freed from the prisons of death and hell that were now closed down by the reign of redemption. With a single phrase Jesus greets all people of good will: 'Peace be with you. My peace I give you, not as the world gives peace.' (Jn 20:19; 14:27) The Church continues to offer this gift of peace. Saint Paul calls Christ *Pax Nostra* (Eph 2:14-16); he is 'our peace' because he reconciled humanity with God and human beings among themselves. By his blood he broke down the walls of hatred, violence, rancour, and resentment, and he sowed justice and love as the essential conditions for peace: 'Love one another.' (Jn 15:12)" (Homily, 6 January 1978)

"The 'No to violence!' must be built firmly on foundations of justice. ... Peace is not the absence of war; peace is not fear of repression; peace is not a balance of two powers based on terror. Peace is the fruit of justice; peace is the flower of love and justice in society. Our 'Yes to peace!' is a 'Yes to God!,' and we would add that our 'Yes to peace!' is also a 'Yes to justice!,' a 'Yes to love!,' and a 'Yes to understanding!' among all. Only in this way can we understand this simple affirmation of peace ... Christ is our peace. ... May those who feel no desire for this peace because of their selfish ways be converted and their hearts filled with love. May those who are far from this peace because their hands are stained with the blood of crimes wash their hands in repentance and realise that there is peace also for sinners and criminals when they repent and love. You are called to be at peace also in your homes. May there be love and reconciliation, and may Christ become present [in everyone and everywhere.]" (Homily, 6 January 1978)

## QUESTIONS FOR REFLECTION

- Thinking about this mystery, what strikes you in light of the message of Scripture and the words of St Oscar Romero?
- Is there a particular intention, or intentions, for which you would like to pray during this decade of the rosary?
- Carry these thoughts and prayers with you as you pray the Our Father, the ten Hail Marys, and the Glory be.

## PRAYER

At the end of this decade, you might wish to pray:

Heavenly Father,
your will for the earth, and for our lives, is peace.
This is the gift of your risen Son.
Help us to work for that justice
which secures peace, a peace that will last.
Inspire us to work for an end to violence, hatred, and war.
We ask this through Christ Our Lord. Amen.

Holy Mary, Mother of God – Pray for us
St Oscar Romero – Pray for us

# POSTSCRIPT

Why is Mary's Motherhood so great? In St Oscar Romero's words:

"It's because she knew how to listen to God's word and put it into practice. It is explained right there in tonight's gospel: after the shepherds left, what did Mary do? Saint Luke captures this intimate scene: 'Mary treasured all these things and pondered them in her heart.' (Lk 2:19) This was Mary's main concern. She humbly recognised that on her own she could never live up to all the greatness of God's plan of salvation, so what she felt was precisely this: 'Behold this smallest servant. He has looked upon my smallness, but despite my smallness, I will offer him all the emptiness of my humility so that he can fill it with the fullness of God.' (Lk 1:38) This is what God hopes that we will do. Therefore, even if we cannot aspire to the perfection of Mary, let us at least imitate the poverty and humility of the shepherds: 'They went back glorifying and praising God for all they had heard and seen; it was just as they had been told.' (Lk 2:20)" (Homily, 31 December 1978)

Over the years, I have read a great deal about Archbishop - now Saint - Oscar Romero. I am drawn to him through biographies and the testimonies of those who knew him; but I am drawn especially by his own writings and, in particular, his powerful sermons. He is a spiritual friend in heaven. We have in common a devotion to Our Lady and a love for the holy rosary. Devotion to the Mother of Jesus mattered to Romero, as he preached in a Homily on 1 January 1978:

> "When devotion to Mary begins to die in our hearts, we have reason to be fearful. It is like the disappearance of the star leading the magi to Christ: we get lost. When devotion to Mary suffers an eclipse, then the light of the divine sun, Christ the Lord, also goes into eclipse. But when there is tenderness and confidence in the hearts of the people and every Christian family, when there is love that prays to Mary, then Christ is near and those souls are not lost."

Romero was a shy man, not without complexity, and of traditional human and spiritual values. First as a priest, and then as a bishop, he always showed concern for the poor. Something shifted within him, however, following the assassination of Fr Rutilio Grande SJ, Manuel Solorzano, and Nelson Lemus. Some claim Romero for the 'right' and others claim him for the 'left,' whether politically or ecclesiastically. Some speak of a radical change, a 'Damascus Road conversion,' at a specific point. Others, more accurately it seems to me, speak of a gradual process of deepening sensitisation and awareness, one which Romero himself described as a strengthening in his pastoral ministry. I have learnt not to label Romero. He belongs to the whole Church and to the whole of humanity. In this sense, with St John Paul II, everyone can say 'He is ours.'

Above all, Romero prioritised shepherding God's people, always remaining faithful to the Gospel and to the Church. God shaped him, over time, to speak and act against the wolves in defence of his sheep, until he finally laid down his life for them in imitation of the Good Shepherd. He calls us to sincere discipleship of the Lord Jesus and to the full proclamation of the Gospel. We are people of the Beatitudes who must announce God's kingdom. We must behave like kingdom-dwellers. When Christ taught us to love and serve others, he really meant us to put it into practice, especially towards those most in need. Love of Christ and love of neighbour mean that defending human life, protecting human dignity, and working for justice and peace, are all integral to our witness. Without them, our discipleship is less than simply incomplete; it is deficient.

Witnessing to the truth is not easy. We may not always, or even often, get it right. However, we look to St Oscar's inspiring example, and we pass it forward to future generations, asking his heavenly intercession.

The final words go to St Oscar Romero, from his Homily on 16 March 1980, a few days before his assassination:

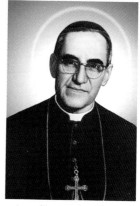

Image of Romero: Bishop and Martyr

"For the Church there is nothing as important as human life and the human person, above all the poor and the oppressed who, besides being human beings, are also divine beings since Jesus said that he takes whatever is done for them as done for himself (Mt 25:40). All that bloodshed and death are beyond any kind of politics. They touch the very heart of God ...

"... I am a minister of this Church of reconciliation, and so I was very happy with the proposal made to me that the Church must not only denounce what is wrong but must also announce hope. One good reason for hope is that the Church's view coincides with the views of many others, and there is therefore a need to begin a sincere dialogue among people with different opinions. I urge everyone, then, not to believe that violence is the only solution, and like Saint Paul, I call everyone to engage in sincere dialogue and to seek reconciliation in God's name."

Heavenly Father,
we give you thanks for the life and witness
of St Oscar Romero, bishop and martyr.
With faithfulness and integrity,
in your Church, and among his people,
he lived and preached
the saving truth of the Gospel of your Son,
our Saviour Jesus Christ.
Renew within us the gift of the Holy Spirit,
so that we too might follow your Son with dedication,
shaping our lives according to his teaching,
announcing the Good News of your mercy and love,
and working for a world where
justice and peace reign for all.
Help us, like St Oscar, to live, think,
and feel with the Church's faith.
May his example deepen our commitment to protect
and serve others, especially the weakest and the poorest.
May it inspire us to put our faith into action
through a practical love towards those most in need.
We ask this through Christ our Lord. Amen

Our Lady, Queen of Peace – pray for us
St Oscar Romero – pray for us

# FURTHER READING & RESOURCES

St John Paul II, Apostolic Letter *Rosarium Virginis Mariae* - On the Most Holy Rosary, 2002. Available in print and online.

Roberto Morozzo Della Rocca, Oscar Romero – Prophet of Hope, Darton, Longman and Todd, London, 2015 – An insightful biography of St Oscar Romero written with balance and clarity.

James R. Brockman SJ, Romero – A Life: The Essential Biography of a Modern Martyr and Christian Hero, Orbis Books, Maryknoll, New York, 2005 – This is a comprehensive and detailed account of St Oscar Romero's life and the context in which he lived as Archbishop of San Salvador.

A Prophetic Bishop Speaks to His People – The Complete Homilies of Archbishop Oscar Arnulfo Romero, Volumes 1 to 6, translated by Joseph Owens SJ, Convivium Press, Miami, 2015 & 2016 – The definitive collection of St Oscar Romero's Homilies while Archbishop of San Salvador, translated into English.

www.romerotrust.org.uk – The website of the Archbishop Romero Trust, which has available online the complete collection of St Oscar Romero's Homilies in English and Spanish, plus his Pastoral Letters, Diary, and other texts. There are also various homilies and lectures about Romero, plus biographical details and videos about him and other martyrs of El Salvador.

www.rcsouthwark.co.uk/diocese/southwark-shrines/national-shrine-to-st-oscar-romero provides images and information about the National Shrine of St Oscar Romero at St George's Cathedral, Southwark.

www.pilgrimways.org.uk/southwark-romero-way provides information about The Romero Way pilgrim route.